The Oldest Young Farmer

THE LIFE OF A LINCOLNSHIRE FARMER

REG DOBBS

First published in the United Kingdom in 2007 by
Sutton Publishing Limited · Phoenix Mill
Thrupp · Stroud · Gloucestershire · GL5 2BU

British Library Cataloguing in Publication Data
A catalogue record for this book is available from the British Library.

ISBN 978-0-7509-4788-6

For Grace
With thanks to Elizabeth for all the 'nitty gritty'

Typeset in Galliard 10.5/13pt.
Typesetting and origination by
Sutton Publishing Limited.
Printed and bound in England.

Contents

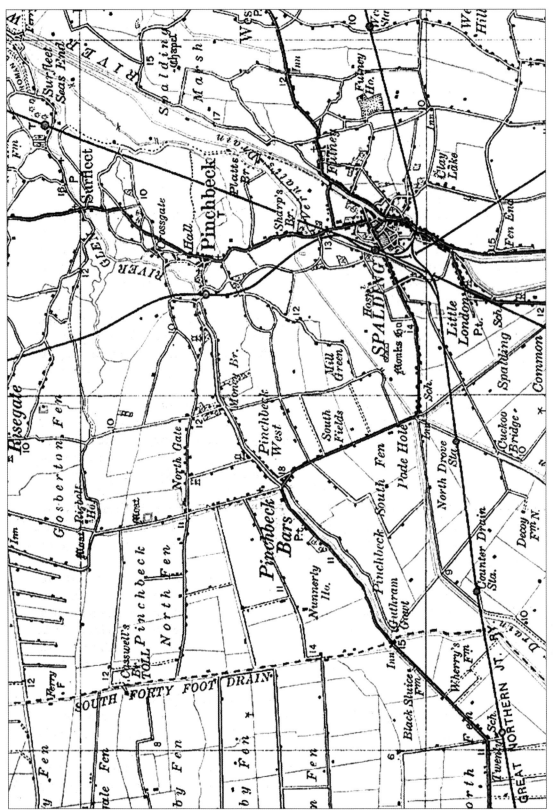

OS Map (1932) showing village location.

Foreword

In my eighty-six years I have been privileged to live through periods of great change in the countryside. Many of the sights of those early days have disappeared. Crafts, skills, indeed a whole way of life have all gone, as have the people who lived by them. New techniques and machines have replaced the old ways and scientific research has taken the place of country lore and the wisdoms handed down from generation to generation.

I was born in 1921 in a period of farm depression and have lived through agricultural boom times when food production was paramount, during the war, for instance, when it was desirable (food from our own resources; to contribute to the trade balance of payments) to the full circle when now crop prices do not cover the costs of production.

The biggest change on the farm has been the replacement of horses by mechanical power. Before 1930 there were a few rare internal combustion tractors. All farm work was done by horse power, ploughing, cultivating, harvesting, carting and much road transport. Some steam engines were used for ploughing and cultivating on large farms and steam tackle was universally used by contractors for thrashing and chaff cutting on even the smallest holdings.

Daily power was provided by heavy horses, often bred on the farm and fuelled by crops grown there, grass, hay, oats, turnips and mangolds. The only purchased fuel was an annual railway truckload of coal for thrashing and house fires, with a gallon or two of paraffin for house lamps and stable lanterns.

Every farm was as self-sufficient as possible. Water came from the well or the cistern which stored rainwater from the house roof. The house cow provided milk and butter for the house and staff. The farm provided food for horses, cattle, pigs, poultry and men. The farmyard had its population of calves, pigs, chickens, ducks and occasionally geese. All of these provided food for the house and with vegetables from the garden, the main foodstuffs bought in were flour, sugar, cheeses, blocks of salt, condiments and tea.

A good farm wife would take the surplus butter, eggs, poultry and fruit to the Buttercross at Spalding Market on Tuesday and use the proceeds to bring home clothes and materials. A good farm wife was independent – that was her household money.

The village was served by local tradesmen. Blacksmiths shoed the horses, sharpened the harrows and mended machinery. Carpenters did the joinery, put up sheds and made coffins when necessary. The miller ground flour and rolled oats for the horses and ground barley for pig meal. The saddler mended harnesses, stuffed collars and saddles and repaired boots. The butcher sold meat for the weekend and travelled round the parish all winter slaughtering the fat pigs which kept the farmers and cottagers in meat in winter and bacon in summer.

Other needs had to be met from the town. The doctor, the vet, the lawyer, the banker, the corn or potato merchant were visited on market day after the cattle market, and the Corn Exchange was a hive of activity in the afternoon.

The village was the centre of social life, school, church, chapel, village cricket and football teams, dances, concerts at a time when transport was limited to pony and trap, pushbike or shanks's pony.

The arrival of bus services and motor cars brought the heady delights of the Regent Cinema within reach on a Saturday night. For people in Spalding the excellent train service meant that London was only an hour and a half away and shopping, shows and even a trip to the theatre were possible.

Perhaps the biggest alteration in lifestyle has been in commuterisation. In my youth almost everyone in the village was employed in agriculture or in businesses that serviced farming. Upwardly mobile youngsters went daily to town as clerks, shopgirls, craftsmen, seeking white collar jobs. Today the farm men are more likely to commute out from town while the farmhouses and cottages are enjoyed by townspeople and businessmen who commute back into town every day; some even commute by train to London from our village.

In the fields in past years we saw gangs of men and women planting potatoes, hoeing weeds, stooking sheaves, carting, picking potatoes; the fields were full of people. Today, except for a few teams cutting vegetables or picking flowers, the only occupant of a field is a lonely tractor driver who has to have the company of a radio programme and his mobile phone.

Economics have swung violently. Fifty years ago there was a living for a farmer on his 50 acres or less. Today only a high-yielding farm of 600 acres or more will provide a living of sorts. Our men quite rightly have a higher standard of living than in the past. In my father's day a man's wage for a week, 37s 6d, was covered by 2 cwt of wheat, the product of one-fifteenth of an acre. Today it takes 4 tonnes of wheat, the crop from an acre or more, to pay a man's wage for one week. So the idyll of a small farm in the country is only there for those rich or lucky enough to be hobby farmers.

The appearance of the village has changed radically over the years. The countryside was half grass for cattle and horses; trees were only planted round stackyards as windbreaks. Every farmstead had cows, pigs and poultry, every cottage its pigsty. The farmyards were burgeoning with huge stacks of wheat, barley and oats, and all potatoes were stored in graves alongside the roads for loading away. It was a pleasant Sunday afternoon ride to go round the village and assess the potato stocks still on hand: shortage or glut?

Now there are many new private houses adding to the council blocks which were first built in 1920. The tiny cottages of the Eight House Row and Blacksmith Row have now gone. There are fewer people working on the farms but many now work in pack houses on the crops from the farms. Many commute to work in Spalding, Peterborough and London, and some townsmen have started reverse commuting, buying a house in the country and selling their house in town. Many have come from further afield as well as London for the cheaper housing.

This change of population and dependence on the motor car have given us all a wider choice of leisure activities and village communal life does not get the support it should. We try to teach our new inhabitants that the fens are not like Hyde Park and that winter is wet and muddy and summer is dusty and smelly. I don't think they are willing to understand.

I have thoroughly enjoyed my eighty-odd years in West Pinchbeck. I carry many happy memories of people, endeavours, the village tulip float, the village Home Guard duties, even skating on the Jockey Drove dyke to the Forty Foot where Father and his mad fen tiger friends skated to Boston and back.

The memories which follow are of days in the open air, tasks and skills now forgotten, people – and the faithful, uncomplaining horses.

R.C. Dobbs
Spring 2007

Note: The photographs in this book belong to my family. The few that do not have been acknowledged but if any error has occurred and I have failed to trace an owner please notify me via the publisher.

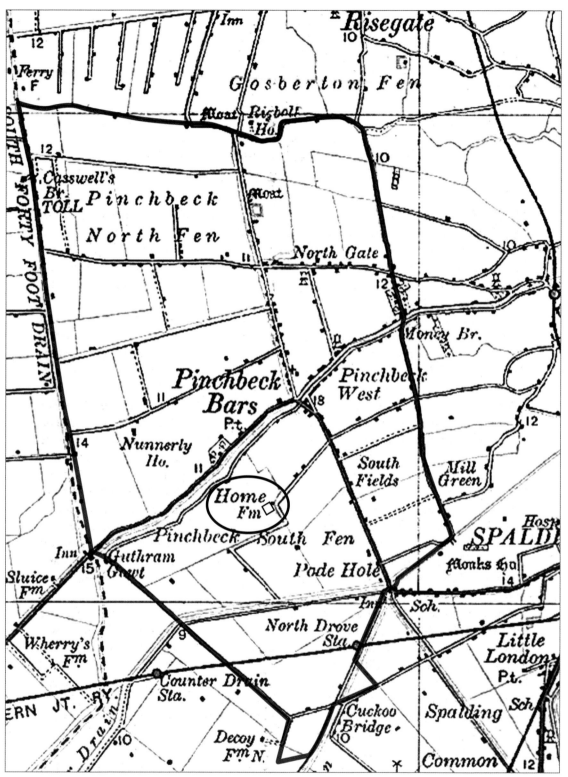

OS Map (1932) showing village/farm location.

1

Farming in the Fens

We have lived through an agrarian revolution. The history books have not yet been written but the changes have been so all-embracing in the last forty years that my grandfather would not recognise our farms today; my father would not be able to manage one and while I think I could manage one without my son's input, I could not operate the sophisticated, hydraulically driven, computer-controlled machinery on the farm today.

The biggest change is in the number employed. Where our small farm of 100 acres needed four full-time people in 1936 with the help of numerous casuals; today, in 2007, we have only five full-time staff on nearly 1,400 acres growing, as well as cereals, some fairly intensive crops (potatoes, sugar beet, daffodil bulbs and forced winter flowers) with casual gang help only at peak periods.

That change and the dramatic mechanisation is visible; what is invisible is the economic change. In the 1930s three or four families would get a living from 100 acres – not a grand living but expectations were low. Today 100 acres will only provide a modest income for one family unless higher returns are gained by very intensive cropping in soft fruit, glasshouse crops, vegetable plant raising or pot plant production. It is possible to generate a high turnover from a nursery (with glasshouses) on a small acreage producing high-value pot plants, propagation material such as plug plants for growing on or large volumes of plants in modules for selling to vegetable producers.

The idyll of the good life on a country smallholding of a few acres has gone, if it ever existed. The small farms that I can recall in my youth provided a very basic living with bread, spread with dripping or margarine and very little jam unless father or mother had another job off the farm.

There is no way that 50 acres of arable crops can sustain the standard of living expected today. Back in the 1930s and even after the Second World War, food was plain and simple. Meat and poultry were a luxury; clothes and furniture were made to last years and the endless expenditure of the consumer society on electrical household equipment, holidays and luxury was as yet undreamed of. It was a make do and mend economy. Patched clothes and darned socks were the norm and, if neat and clean, quite acceptable. The repair shops and cobblers were always busy. Father used to assess the applicants for a job by looking at their trousers: 'Worn at the knees – good; worn at the backside – no good.'

At that time there were many small farms and smallholdings in the village. The large ones run by H.B. Atkinson, the Banks and Holmes families and A.K. Wright had many cottages and employed men from the village. Many of the smaller farms were employing three or four men full time with extra help at harvest and thrashing. Few women were on the land as regular employees but almost all who were able helped out with spring potato planting. They used to turn up in long skirts, aprons, heavy boots and cotton bonnets to earn pin money. In the social pecking order of the day, they rated below the shopgirls and the women in domestic service, though many would claim to be merely helping out as a favour to the farmer.

The farms were almost self-sufficient in food. The poultry on the holdings provided eggs and meat; the universal pigs provided fresh pork, bacon and ham; every farm had a cow or several. Variety came from ducks, geese, the occasional guineafowl and, of course, rabbits galore.

A few traditional dishes still existed. Every year in midsummer the rooks nesting in the surrounding trees had to be culled and the breasts of the young ones were used to prepare a delicious pie. In season we used to catch eels with a long-handled gleave, a barbed fork with four or five blades, from the drain just past the farm. We had to say we enjoyed them, fried for supper, but they were tougher than old bicycle tyres and would have been better stewed. Another seasonal dish was the huge pan-sized horse mushrooms gathered from the paddock of an autumn morning.

All these dishes were a treat because of their novelty. This is something missing in life today. The pleasure of fruit newly in season, rhubarb, gooseberries, strawberries, raspberries, currants, each one a novelty in turn. One of the culinary delights was Whit Sunday lunch with the first new potatoes with fresh mint and tender young peas! Today these items are available all the year round from the deep freeze or supermarket – but without the thrill.

The equipment on the farms was pretty basic. It had not altered much in a hundred years. The innovation of steam power was making big strides on the larger farms where pairs of steam engines were used for cable ploughing and heavy cultivating but steam engines were only used on small farms for driving thrashing tackle and chaff cutters. Even hay baling was done by hand in a portable press brought to the haystacks.

One big steam-powered machine which enjoyed a short vogue in the late 1930s was the gyrotiller. This machine rotated long tines in the soil to a depth of 30 inches or more. It gave a thorough cultivation, broke up the plough pan and was going to double crop yields. Unfortunately the huge lumps of clod were intractable in a dry spell or turned into a bottomless mud swamp in wet weather. Gyrotillers sank without trace.

Tractors had begun to make an appearance on farms after 1918. In the 1930s Henry Ford saw the potential for oil-powered tractors in the US prairies and began to produce a tractor to supplement the Model T Ford car and meet the competition from the Case, Oliver, Minneapolis Moline and Allis Chalmers tractors. The model produced for the UK market did not run on petrol like the American models. It used kerosene and was merely started on petrol until warm. Our first iron-wheeled Fordson, bought in 1938, was at first used for ploughing and heavy cultivating. Before long it was used to tow the binder, the grass cutter and a variety of hastily adapted horse equipment. Gradually it ousted the horse which we thought would always be needed for light cultivation and carting. By 1960 our last carthorses were gone: Punch, Jolly, Prince, Blossom and Metal, all old faithful friends. Now we have a fleet of TW 15s and 7740s – not quite the same.

In those early days we all grew a wide range of crops. Pasture grass, clover and ryegrass for 'seeds' hay, oats and mangolds or swedes for animal feed. A proportion of the barley was ground at the Glenside Mill by Harold Garfoot or later Stan Hall to feed the pigs, and the wheat tailings and more went to feed the poultry.

The major grain crop was wheat, which suited the bodied soils on the farm, and the major cash crops in roots were potatoes and sugar beet. At various times and with mixed degrees of success we grew peas and beans, for harvesting dry, for the fresh market and for canning.

Early ventures of an experimental nature to make that quick fortune were linseed, grass seed, brassicas, sprouts and cauliflower, canary grass for birdseed during the war, onions and a fair acreage of beet seed. The beet seed contract led to an interesting sortie into flower seed growing for a couple of years – larkspur. This needed cutting and drying in sheaves. The thrashing of less than half an acre was a biblical operation with a home-made flail on a sheet spread on the barn floor. This was not a positive kind of action and we ended by bashing handfuls of stems against a fine mesh potato riddle. Imported seeds were impossible at that time but now all those seeds are grown in dryer climates.

This interest in flowers led to a small start in tulip growing in the less controlled days after 1945. Daffodils were added when we began winter forcing in 1960. Today we can follow the husbandry of virtually any crop in the country but in an age of specialisation where large investments in designated equipment are needed we have reduced our major cropping to wheat, beet, potatoes and daffodils. The tulips proved labour-intensive and uneconomic and have gone. The brassicas and onion crops (leeks and bunching salad onions) are leased out on contract.

The capital needed to properly equip for a crop is shown by the cost of setting up to handle our crop of less than 100 acres of potatoes. At today's costs this adds up to over £150,000. We can only justify this investment by taking on contract work and putting the tackle to multiple use in the daffodil crop.

These sorts of budgets, gross margins and calculations did not exist in those early days. It was possible to start farming with the simplest of equipment. My father started on 30 acres in Jockey Drove in 1920 with a horse, a plough and a set of harrows. His brother was sent with a drill to help sow the first crops and slowly other tools were added. For ploughing, the all-steel Howard or Ransome semi-digger ploughs were preferred. For cultivating, heavy and light sets of zigzag harrows were used. The design of the cup feed seed drills had not altered for generations and the trusty Smythe and Coultas makes continued until the steel-bodied force feed US models became available, designed for work behind tractors after the war.

The emphasis was on hand work. Manpower was cheap. Equipment had to be bought with money, and money was in short supply. All countrymen were skilled with hand tools, and calloused hands proved that they used them. We spent days with a hand hoe chopping thistles out of the grain crops; the hoe was drawn between every potato down the row and each sugar beet row was thoroughly hand hoed twice after being gapped and singled. Our only concession to mechanisation was the horsehoe – where a boy led a horse in the shafts of the horsehoe which was steered by the man behind, cutting an A hoe in between the rows of corn half the width of the drill breed. The same hoe with L-blades in addition was adapted to horsehoe between the wider rows of sugar beet.

The potatoes were grown in 28-inch rows and needed a deeper tilth. The land was opened out with a ridging plough or a three-row ridger. The fertiliser was sown along the open furrows. This would be guano from Chile and later mixed compound fertiliser (ground rock phosphate, sulphate of potash and sulphate of ammonia), often mixed on the barn floor. The potato setts were planted by hand and the ridges split back to cover the seed. Potatoes were regarded as the cleaning crop and cultivations would begin with harrowing the ridges flat and hilling them up several times. The gutters between the rows were skerried with a one-horse cultivator so close to the rows that 'the seed turned round twice'. In the midst of all this activity the hand hoe chopped through between every potato just before the final ridging so that the land was clean of weeds for the next crop.

My recollections of those days is of hand tools, hoes, spades, scythes, all immaculately cared for, sharp and oiled, large gangs of men hoeing across large fields, exchanging banter and gossip. There was a bit of cut and cover as Stan Hubbert, a very skilled hoeman, said 'You never want to let a few weeds get you behind' as I struggled to keep up.

And the blisters. The skin on our hands was half an inch thick but every new job would raise a crop of blisters. The hoes of early summer would change to four-tine muck forks as we emptied muck from the cattle yards. Everything on the farm had to be loaded and unloaded by human muscle. At the beginning of July the forks changed to two-tine handforks for hay turning, heaping and carting.

A welcome change before harvest was a few days with a lunch bag and bottle of drink carrying a scythe on the river banks. We used to rent the banks and slipes for grazing the bullocks and apart from the continual fencing, our bank manager (the garth man!) needed help to mow down the nettles and thistles, huge Scotch thistles that grew there. Father used to exhort us: 'Cut 'em in July, they will surely die', so we used to slash at them and run back lest the prickly brutes fell over on us.

All this was good practice for mowing out the dykes and round the wheat fields to make an opening for the horses to pull the binder. Some time in the year before the autumn work took precedence, hedge knives were brought out, sharpened and given a trim. There is an art in sharpening with a whetstone. A scythe has a very thin blade and can be fettled up with a few strokes once sharpened but a hedge knife has a thick blade, is put to heavy chopping and can hit hidden barbed wire. It is difficult but essential to keep a good edge on a hedge knife. The trick to keeping a good impenetrable hedge is always to chop it upwards. A lazy trimmer will chop downwards because it is easier but the twig bases are broken off and the hedge soon becomes gappy. A good thorn hedge is one that has been trimmed upwards leaving twigs neatly cut, not broken, and with plenty of buds for regrowth. The modern flail mower does a rough job but since hedge trimming is merely an unpaid park-keeper's duty on the farm for appearance's sake, it probably does not matter much.

The one hand tool I have omitted so far is the most blistering of them all – the spade. We spent a lot of time with a spade. A lot of winter days were spent in the dykes doing them out. We all had our favourites. The narrow-bladed Crocker was ideal for deep digging and clay cutting. The Linden was broader and was used for steady digging on silt or heavy soils. No-one liked a new spade. It was thick and heavy. They worked easiest when half worn, thin and brightly oiled up every night. We had ample opportunity to get acquainted. The hundreds of yards of potato heaps had to be covered with earth one spit deep in October and a second covering to a foot thick before winter. As the trench alongside the clamp deepened it seemed a long way to the top of the heap. If the going was easy with plenty of small clods in the trench a small pan shovel was used to top off the soiling up. The pan shovel was light, sharp and could deliver more soil for less effort!

Today we employ fewer workers on the farm except for rush periods yet we provide employment for large numbers of people manufacturing and servicing our machines, making and distributing plant foods and medicines, making packaging materials, for people packing and processing our product and for hosts of hauliers moving huge volumes of material on and off the farm.

Our farm workers now enjoy a much higher standard of living than anyone could dream of fifty years ago. The material luxuries of modern household equipment are enjoyed by everyone, refrigerators, TV, videos, electric washers and cleaners are all standard. All our workers have a car. All take long (by 1950 standards) holidays paid to my mystification at a rate greater than if they were working. All except one of our staff take holidays abroad now, flying or cruising.

All this is a wonderful change from the penury and deprivation of the 1930s and '40s. Father who laboured to build up the business could only afford to go overseas when the king and war office sent him to India. I don't think he would comprehend the changes that have taken place. He would understand that that early tractor driver of his, a greasy misfit of an oilrag at first, would take pride of place eventually over the head waggoner with his shiny leggings. He would probably accept the loss of the foreman on the large fen farm riding round on his bicycle, supervising, wearing his bowler hat. He would understand that the foreman or farm manager would have to become a 'hands on' person taking his turn on the combine or sprayer. But would he understand that the farmer too on a 500-acre farm in these straitened times would have to be a full-time operative, doing his business and market trading by mobile telephone from a tractor seat or in touch with the driver of a machine with a breakdown in the far field by radio?

In our early days we had no office. If a letter needed writing, mother wrote it. Men did not mess about with office work. But after the war the Inland Revenue decided that the past systems of block taxation under Schedule B with excess profits taxed at 100% was not good enough, so even small farms had to start book-keeping and hire an accountant to present the annual balance sheet.

Gradually our office system improved or increased to cope with double entry ledgers, annual stocktaking and the rest. More recently PAYE and VAT and legislation on Health and Safety, CoSHH, Food Safety and traceability, field records have meant that an undue amount of effort has to be devoted to recording every small deed on the farm, be it the changing of oil in a tractor or the placing of mice bait. I was taught that the best fertiliser for a field was the farmer's foot. Today I am sure that is still true but if the farmer has got his finger stuck in a computer keyboard his foot can be a long way from the trouble shooting that is needed.

These great changes in country and village life have come about in a mere forty years. It has all been made possible by the greater revenue to agriculture from higher wheat prices. Living conditions bear no comparison to life before 1950. Most farm workers' houses are fitted with inside plumbing and many have central heating; all are connected to mains services of water and electricity. Farm workers now enjoy privileges that their grandparents only hoped for – rights of employment, minimum wage levels, unemployment benefit, sick pay and holiday benefits greater than our American cousins.

These are all wonderful changes for the better. If there are any clouds on the horizon, there is a big question as to whether the lower prices for farm crops and livestock now beginning can sustain the higher standards of living enjoyed by everyone. Will the level of bureaucracy hamstring and drive out the keen producers who are more skilled at husbandry than administration? Can the value of the output afford the escalating armies of inspectors, controllers and hangers-on? Certainly grandfather would say it could not.

One certain fact is here to stay. Forty years ago farming and working in agriculture was a 'way of life'. Today the pace has speeded up; the pressures build up on every facet of the job. Stress is now the daily companion of the farmer as much as the factory manager.

I have tried to create the impression that before 1939 money was scarce on the small farms. My neighbour Harold Christian and his father Harry have kept records of the prices for their crops for two generations. In 1936 they sold wheat to G.F. Birch for 38s 6d per qr. of 4½ cwt and later 22s (which is 5s per cwt).

In 1939 wheat was only 31s 6d per quarter.

Potatoes in the period 1936 to 1939 varied from £2 10s to £3 5s, rising in 1944 to £6 or £7 per ton for King Edward and Majestic.

Sugar Beet	1943	£3 per ton
Wheat	1956/7	£24 per ton
	1960	£18 " "
	1970	£25–£30 per ton
	1974	£48 per ton
	1979	£75–£100 per ton
	1980	£110–£120 per ton
	1998	£70–£80 per ton

The price for 2006 harvest wheat was quoted at £75 to £80 per ton.

2

My Village, West Pinchbeck

I was born in 1921 in Jockey (now Starlode) Drove, West Pinchbeck, on Proctors Farm. At the end of the First World War two large farms were split up into smallholdings of about 30 acres and rented out by the Holland County Council to returning ex-servicemen. My father, Cecil, had served in India and Mesopotamia in the Royal Artillery and was successful in getting one of the holdings. He married Rose Mary Alexander, a comely girl from further along the Jockey Drove, who was in service in Boston. They had no money and Grandfather Walter Dobbs helped them start by lending a corn drill and a few implements.

As English villages go, West Pinchbeck is relatively new. Before 1800 it was a sparsely populated fenland area, poorly drained, with bad roads, and farming and businesses servicing agriculture the only occupations. Half the land was in grass for cattle and horses and half in arable crops. The cattle were walked to market and a lot of the wheat was loaded on barges to go along the Forty Foot Drain to Boston or later carted by horse and waggon to the new-fangled railway stations at Pinchbeck, North Drove or Spalding.

The district fell within the area of Canon Wayet, Vicar of Pinchbeck. He recognised that the far-flung fens needed pastoral care and at his own expense built the church of St Bartholomew in 1850. A Methodist chapel on the Glenside was added and later the Northgate chapel was built.

In my father's youth there was much rivalry between church and chapel and between the communities at the 'Jockey' and the 'Bars'. The church became very much a social centre for the village. The school behind it provided education for all village children, both Methodist and C of E, and additions of a chapel and schoolroom at Pode Hole and a school at Dunsby Fen completed the cover of this fen. Services were held at both Pode Hole and Dunsby Fen and on great occasions like the church Sunday School feast children from Pode Hole joined in at St Bartholomew's and decorated farm waggons pulled by beribboned horses brought up the children from Dunsby Fen.

The church provided clubs for young men of the parish and I can recall magic lantern shows, concerts, dances and whist drives in the school until the late 1950s, and football matches on Harold Smith's grassfield at the Peacock public house and cricket matches on Tom Peach's grassfield next to the blacksmith.

Life in the countryside was tough in my youth. Houses outside the village had nothing. No water supply; drinking water had to be drawn from a cistern which

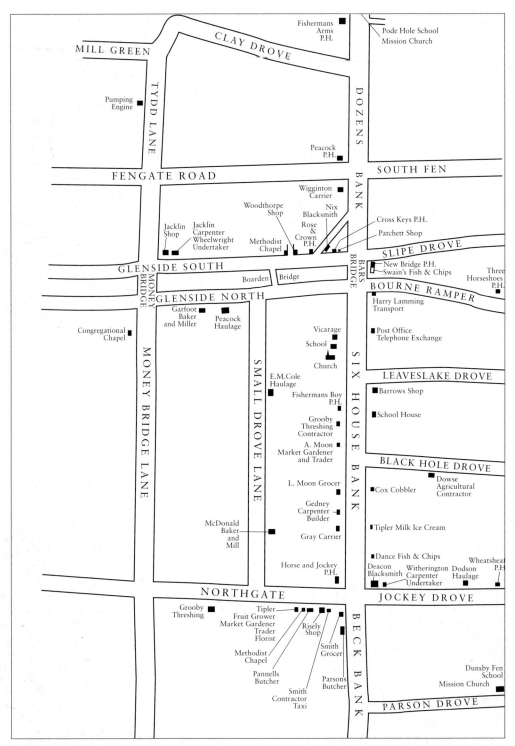

West Pinchbeck village in the 1930s. (M.K. Chappell)

St Bartholomew's Church, West Pinchbeck, c. 1950.

St Bartholomew's Church, 2006.

The old West Pinchbeck Primary School next to the church. The building is now the Village Hall.

collected the roof water and passed it through a charcoal filter. In dry summers we had to cart water for livestock from the river.

Houses and cottages were lit by oil lamps and candles. Embroidery, letter writing and study had to be at the kitchen table under the best oil lamp, and winter work in the barn and stables depended on hurricane lamps. Electricity was available in the village itself but the countryside was pitch dark until rural electrification brought a supply to all the outlying farms in the 1950s. Before then all cooking was done on the coal-fired kitchen ranges or specially bought paraffin or bottled gas stoves. Wash day (Monday) meant getting up early to light the copper and trundle out the dolly tub.

When we went from the smallholding in Jockey Drove to Brightman's farm in Hollands Chase in 1930 we had no piped water, no telephone, no electricity and not even a daily post. Letters and packages were left at the Peacock on the main road. Gradually these services reached rural areas. Perhaps the most striking was the telephone. We were connected in about 1936 and were instantly in touch with businesses and relatives anywhere in the country. For the first year or two we used to shout on long distance calls.

The village was well catered for by eight pubs and alehouses; today only one, the Fishermans Arms, remains.

In my early days in Jockey Drove I saw little of the neighbours, except the Coatens whose son Harris joined me in exploring hedges and dykes, trees and birds' nests. The nearest neighbours were the Dodsons with their lorries; next door was Mrs Gladys Dodson who kept the books. Next along was Mrs Atkin, a widow with a blind son Tom, very talented musically, who went away to become a cathedral organist.

Then came the Maddisons and Kirlews and Gentleman John Seymour. Mr Seymour was remarkable in our workaday community for always appearing in a suit and collar and tie as befitted his position as the local Prudential agent. Kirlew, a stocky old timer, I shall always recall as the person I knocked down with my bike as he walked in the middle of the road in the fog on a pitch black night as I went for my music lesson. The lesson was given by John Christian who lived next door to Riseley's shop. He worked on the roads all day, taught piano in the evenings and played at the chapel on Sundays. 'The Harmonious Blacksmith' still brings a glimpse of his firm fingers authoritatively hammering away as he patiently tried to instil new mysteries in my thick head.

We lived in a conclave of smallholders, most of them settled on the land as ex-servicemen in 1920. On Proctor's farm in our lane were Tommy Wheatley, Harry Branton, Tom Boothby, Fisher, Eddie Gotobed, Charlie Alexander, my uncle, and further down, Len Shotbolt.

In Leaveslake Drove another farm had been split up into holdings and there were settled Bob Christian, the father of one of my school pals, Cecil, and host to some good Christmas parties where the youngsters did their own thing while the old ones played cards and smoked and drank, also Len Cook, Darley, Waltham (one arm, three daughters), Harold Chappell before he moved to Glenside and my uncle Charlie Dobbs. We shared resources with Uncle Charlie and during the days when we pooled horses and carts to carry and stack the grain harvest, I got my rudimentary training in farming and muscle power. Charlie was noteworthy because while we all had a cow or two for house milk and butter he milked half a dozen cows for the dairy trade. His wife, Aunt Ciss (Marvin), was the daughter of a foreman on a large farm. She was reputed to have filled, riddled, bagged and weighed 5 tons of potatoes in a day single-handed – yet she was still quiet and ladylike. It was a hard life down on those fens but Charlie always had a smile and a laugh for us young ones.

There were a few jobbing builders about and house builders, like Bill Gedney, but the one I saw the most of in those early days was Albert Burrell, a real rough diamond who repaired our roofs and pointed our walls to keep us going when we had little money to build new. He was the village cricket umpire and perhaps the twelfth man in the team. His daughter Millie had the sweetest soprano voice in the church choir, renowned for miles round.

In my early days the Blacksmith Row consisted of a terrace of about six tiny cottages. The most memorable occupant here was Grandma Waite (always called Grammy) who kept tabs on the village, and was always to be seen in majestic progress on her three-wheeled bicycle.

A little further along on Dozens Bank where Cis Gotobed's petrol pumps and lorry yard later stood was the Eight House Row, a line of joined up cottages which could only have been one up and one down. In one of these cottages lived the Hunt family. They had half a dozen children and we speculated wildly about sleeping arrangements. The only solution we could come up with was that the boys were put to bed two at a time and when asleep were stood up in the corner to make room for the rest. I went to school with Charlie Hunt and a crowd of boys dressed in short pants made of brown corduroy which really smelt rank when it got warm. We all had shoes or boots of a sort but the Ingle boys from Money Bridge were hard put to for shoe leather and often had a fresh air patch at the back of their trousers. Some of those youngsters stayed nearly all their lives in the village, the Haresigns, Bunny Leverton, Harris Coaten, Harold Christian, Ron and Chris Cooling, Laurence Tipler, Somerfield, 'Booker' Strickson and the Gotobeds.

In our new farm in Hollands Chase we had as neighbours John J. Twell, the foreman for Frank Richardson of Morton. J.J. was a very capable foreman on 300 acres, running beef cattle, grain and potatoes, handling a large gang of Irish workers every harvest until November and gradually changing from horse to tractor power. I was told he had had his own small farm but could not make it pay; this large one however was well run.

Next was Harry Christian. Not always the first to get his work done, Harry bought his first car, a Ford 8, and like all the farmers used to shout 'Whoa' for it to stop. One foggy night he turned off the ramper (high, dry road) down into the lane and turned a bit too hard and went head first into the dyke. Next morning, red-faced, he pulled it out with a horse and towed it home.

On the other side was Charlie Cooling. He was a much misunderstood man. He and his cheerful wife worked hard on about 25 acres and raised two girls and three boys. He had a reputation for being mean as muck and would go in the Peacock on a Saturday night, buy half a pint and make it last until closing time. He smoked a pipe and even locked up his matches. His wife had to take the eggs and butter to the Butter Cross to sell and bring back margarine and groceries for her family. Money didn't exist in those days. But Charlie Cooling took over the little farm from his father who had drunk it into debt. By scrupulously careful management (or do you call it meanness?) he paid off the debts and the copyhold on the land before he died.

We seemed to attract a few older workers who, it was said, had had the steel worn out of them, though they served us well. Bobby Gay, an ex-horseman, came to help in our last years with horses. He was rough as soot but good natured.

For over fifty years the part of Pinchbeck parish known as Money Bridge was renowned for its stud of Percheron heavy horses. The Sneath family was brought up with horse blood in their veins as their father George Edward (Ted) built up the fame of his Percheron horses nationwide and even internationally. They were shown in the ring at the national horse show annually at Peterborough and even appeared at the Wembley horse show. Admirers came from all over and satisfied buyers took the offspring to improve their bloodlines among enthusiasts all over the country. Some even went to the USA, Pakistan and Australia.

An evening at Money Bridge Manor House would evoke days now long past as Ted and his wife, over cups of tea (no strong drink), recalled show successes and pointed out the proudly displayed sideboards and shelves laden with silver cups and trophies. In proudest place of all was a ceramic replica of Saltmarsh Silver Crest, the great national breed champion, whose likeness was created by Doris Lidner for Royal Worcester and issued as a one-off issue of 500 pieces, with the No. 2 model coming to Ted Sneath, the owner. This stallion was entered in the *Guinness Book of Records* as the heaviest horse in the country.

The stud travelled its stallions round the district for years with groom Bob Adams. The champion entires, of course, were in demand to serve other bloodlines of the same breed.

My own connection with the Money Bridge Percherons came through another Edward Sneath, the eldest son. He was very much involved with breaking in, working, and training the young horses to work in gears (trait chains) on the plough and harrows and in shafts on carts and drays. It was only natural that he did the showing, even after he started farming on his own at Leaveslake Drove. I had been at school with young Ed and we both started farming at about the same time. It helped that our wives had been workmates and were still close friends.

Who of our present folk will be remembered in two generations time? Maybe Jim Peach, farmer, sportsman and painter, Stuart Carter, blacksmith, Gordon Tansley, farm labourer and dartsman, Trevor Sneath, contractor, Alice Cook, churchwarden, Maurice Chappell or his brother Councillor Bryn. Who knows?

3

Grandfather Walter

Grandfather Walter Dobbs sat in his wooden armchair for days on end in his latter years, wearing a shiny dark grey serge suit and bright black leather boots, a real Edwardian. Here he would receive visitors and his sons and grandchildren to discuss day-to-day farming problems, castigate markets and offer advice from his ninety years of experience.

Whenever he went to church or on business to market he enhanced his patriarchal appearance by wearing a black bowler hat. I remember it well because as a schoolboy I borrowed it for a dare to walk through the town centre at midday. No-one gave me a second glance.

Grandfather Walter Dobbs by stacks.

He had lived in the village of West Pinchbeck all his life and so far as I am aware he never went away. He must have done once because his last house was named after the Wembley Exhibition where he and Grandma Caroline bought some of the furnishings for it.

He was born in 1864, one of two sons of Peter, a small farmer, at Model Farm, Dozens Bank, in the heyday of Queen Victoria. He must have been a local 'go-getter'. He set eyes on the pretty local schoolmistress, Caroline Osman, wooed her and wed her.

They raised six boys and two girls in the tough times before the First World War. There was not enough room for all those young men on the farm so Walter was apprenticed to Wilkinson, a Spalding cabinet maker, and his brother Les to an ironmongery business. Work in Canada sparked a lot of interest pre-war and my father Cecil and my uncle Walter emigrated to help farming on the prairies and build the Canadian Pacific Railway or whatever fortune cast before them.

After the outbreak of war Cecil, Walter and Les joined up for the duration and the younger boys, Fred, Charles and Harold, helped on the farm. Grandfather carefully tutored them and husbanded his savings to help the boys start their own small farms of about 25 acres. Times had improved during the war and out of his savings he was able to pay off the copyhold on Model Farm where he lived and build Wembley House in 1926 in a 4-acre paddock for retirement.

Harold took over Model Farm across the road; Fred moved into the 24-acre holding in Slipe Drove and Charles and Cecil (now demobilised) became tenants in county council smallholdings in Leaveslake and Jockey Drove. Leslie went to Sutton Bridge to start an agricultural engineering business and Walter, who had enlisted in Canada, was demobilised there and made his way to California, house building and making film sets in Los Angeles.

With the family off his hands it was time for Grandfather Walter to retire. Still a healthy 62 years old he kept bullocks on his grass field and on the Slipe riverbank and travelled round to see his sons in a big red sit-up-and-beg Morris Oxford, advising and keeping them in order.

Christmas was a great feast. After milking and feeding the hens and livestock we cycled up to Wembley House to partake of a huge turkey and Christmas pudding for dinner and jellies, cakes and a big Christmas cake for tea. I had been warned to be on my best behaviour as the grown-ups, father and Uncle Les, talked in the parlour. Christmas Day was for the senior sons; the younger ones ate the left-overs on Boxing Day. When I tired of the toy or book I had brought I would go to Aunt Dorothy who had a soft spot for me and would take me into the kitchen for the treats in the pantry till it was time to go, half asleep, home.

In those last years visits from family meant a lot to him and grandmother. He would sit in his armchair and look up the road to see his sons on their way home from work or market, disappointed if they did not call in. I was often deputed to run small errands there and remember calling in my work clothes, only to find that Aunt Dot, who was looking after them, was walking backward before me, laying down sheets of newspaper even though I had brushed my boots on arrival. Thus I was ushered into the presence. A rare treat was to watch him smoke the occasional

Grandfather Walter Dobbs in his Sunday best in front of Wembley House.

cigarette – carefully puffing down to the last half inch and then finishing it off on the point of a pin!

Grandfather Walter retired too early but his sons were hungry to take over. He retired on his savings and was regarded as comfortably off. But I imagine he lived too long and inflation eroded his income. To me he always evokes the image of wealth – and the lessons of money's transitory nature. He used to have a soft linen bag in his pocket for gold sovereigns. He had started farming on the gold standard; he went through change to paper money and devaluations. I still have one of his golden half sovereigns to bring me back to earth if I get a financial rush of blood to the brain. He always comported himself with dignity and gravity – perhaps as a result of serving for many years as a churchwarden. The family placed a stained-glass window in the north wall of our church to commemorate his service.

My grandfather taught me many things: patience, understanding, to endure hard labour because the time or weather was right. 'The difference between a good farmer and a bad one is a fortnight.' He taught me to husband my efforts and few possessions. One of his many maxims was 'Bodge and stay; build and run away'. Still true today. His foot would feel the soil and judge it ready to harrow or drill or plant

Reginald Cecil Dobbs aged three.

Reg aged four.

Cecil William Dobbs and son Reg, aged six.

Father and Mother with son Reg, aged six.

with potatoes. He taught me to appreciate the land we occupy for a short time and that I should strive to leave it better than I found it. And if I count my pennies twice or smoke my panatellas a bit low – it must be in my genes.

My introduction to country life started on the council smallholding. Wives and children were encouraged to help and my first effort at turning hay with a two-tine hand fork at the age of three saw me stick the rusty fork through my shoe and foot and beat an ignominious retreat.

Other adventures included being found one evening in the stable standing as a toddler between the back legs of a shire horse with my arms round his legs. Quietly coaxed away by father with 'Good boy' and 'Steady Prince', murmured so gently and probably in desperate relief.

Another day, helping the thrashing gang on the corn stack, I ventured too near the edge and slipped off, to land with my spine on a hard wooden cart taildoor. It felt like the end of the world but I dared not complain.

So I grew from an undersized runt of a baby cradled at first in a small chest of drawers to an ungainly schoolboy. The fields, the grass paddocks, the hedges were the playground for me and Harris Coaten. We discovered the magic of birds' nests and tadpoles, the mystery of our secret dykes and the hugeness of the animals, the cows and horses.

All memories of that small farm are bright. The sun shone on the fields. The weather was always wonderful; I remember one particularly hot harvest day when we all sat on the grass under the big tree in the yard for our tea, new home-made bread and butter, warm tomatoes and hot sweet tea. Even the winters were crisp as we put on our pattens and skated along the dykes!

4

The Kitchen

The hub of the farm was the farmhouse kitchen. In 1930 it was a large sparse bleak room. It had a thick painted door fastened with heavy bolts and a huge iron key. The door opened into a room with coarse brick walls thick with a greenish distemper and a red-tiled floor. For the first few years the transition from outside, cold, wet and windy, to inside, warmer but draughty, was sudden because the door opened directly into a small paved yard where a low timber and corrugated iron shed held supplies of coal, wood and baskets of dry kindling fetched from the kid stack (a large heap of twigs and sticks stored from tree and hedge trimming) in the horse paddock. The garden path led behind this shed to the privy (a two-seater earth closet) and to the stables and crew yard.

After a few months of winter the proximity of the great outdoors whistling through the back door caused the small yard to be enclosed with a structure called the veranda, well endowed with windows, which kept the winds, storming directly across the North Sea from Siberia, at bay. This luxurious addition provided room to hang up some of the work coats and store the gumboots and waterproofs which cluttered the kitchen wall immediately behind the door. The veranda also helped on washdays to accommodate the dolly tub and peg nearer to the copper of boiling water in the outside shed. This copper was always kept beautifully clean. Heated by a stick and coal fire underneath, it was used to boil the 'whites' and provide hot water for the washing, for bathnight and for such special occasions as the ritual scalding of the pig.

Inside the kitchen improvements came along at regular intervals. The big shallow yellow glazed sink under the window was supplied with water by a simple leather valved pump from the cistern, which was filled with rainwater from the house roof and if carefully used it rarely ran dry. The horses and cattle were watered from a well at the bottom of the garden and in very dry summers the water table dropped so that we had to borrow a horsedrawn water cart and fetch cattle water from the nearest drain with a supply. There was constant pressure to modernise the sink and soon the old pump was replaced by a shiny red painted semi-rotary which did not need priming before it would spout water.

In about 1935 a big change came, the connection to the water company's mains supply almost a mile away at the ramper road. Just imagine! Clean running water at the turn of a tap. Before then all drinking water had to be filtered through a big stone filter filled with charcoal. This roof water had its own unique taste. I suppose it tasted of charcoal but I always imagined the sparrows perching on the roof added a little *je ne sais quoi*. No wonder the water was mostly drunk boiled in tea or cocoa.

The kitchen contained a couple of wooden chairs, a work table, a dresser for storing basins, dishes and jugs and at the side of the chimney breast a cupboard for saucepans, frying pans, roasting tins and – most essential   a supply of candles, matches and candle holders for lighting our way upstairs. The light was an oil lamp with a wick which needed trimming nightly and in the veranda hung the hurricane lanterns which were used to light the stables, the barn or the cowshed whenever we had to work in the dark.

The kitchen was the place where meals were prepared. The original cooker was a cottage range which consisted of a coal fireplace with an oven on one side and a water boiler on the other. This was filled from a water can and the hot water drawn off from a tap at the bottom. The whole of the grate was kept clean and shining by black-leading it – smoke went up the chimney if the wind was right and ashes were shovelled out from below the firebars. It was a daily chore; laying the fire, cleaning it out and getting a kettle on the boil before breakfast. Even in the hottest of weather the fire had to be lit for cooking, tea making and for the odd farm task such as heating branding irons. This was the situation in the early 1930s. Later we improved to a paraffin fuelled cooker which was quicker to start in the mornings and less temperamental when the wind direction changed. Life became almost three star when we discovered the luxury of cooking on a calor gas stove. To this day we still have a reserve calor gas ring in the washhouse which is pressed into use when the electricity supply fails.

In later years some cooking was done in the next room, a large living room, when the range was exchanged for a Raeburn unit, a sort of poor man's Aga, which combined an open fire, a smartly tiled oven with hot compartment above and a hot water boiler behind which supplied the domestic hot water needs. This room contained a large wooden armchair for the man of the house, a large table covered with a heavy cloth in entertaining mode, oilcloth in work mode or white linen for meals. The floor covering was pieces of carpeting of better quality than the peg rugs of the kitchen, though for years the hearthrug in the living room was a large heavy peg rug made during the long winter nights from snipped up old clothes.

Entertainment was provided by the Cossor wireless which was powered by a large dry battery and wet accumulators which had to be taken every week for recharging. I remember as a very small boy the wonder of the faint whispering of voice and music from a crystal set. But by the 1930s everyone had a smart bakelite wireless set with a long aerial spanning the chimney and garden. This kept us in touch with the world; news of events in London, football matches, deaths and crowning of kings and weather forecasts. Miles out in the fens we were able to enjoy Dame Nellie Melba, Henry Hall and Jack Payne with the latest dance tunes, thrill to Gracie Fields or laugh with *ITMA*.

The wireless made life either enjoyable or endurable during the long evenings under the oil lamp. It was hard work to decipher the newspaper until we got an Aladdin paraffin lamp with an incandescent mantle, which was set in the middle of the table and made it possible to read and to write a few letters. Father had a beautiful copperplate hand but I never saw him write a letter. As a practical farmer he had an aversion to letter writing, and perhaps a healthy distrust of over-clever clerks and lawyers.

A central passageway ran through the centre of the house to the front door, a huge timber construction graced by a massive round black door knob that would unfasten

Mother in full apron for kitchen chores.

the door, and the door could be opened, but the only time I saw it unbarred and unbolted was when new furniture came into the house or a coffin departed. On the other side of the passage was the front room. On a working farm this chamber was rarely used. I can only recall it being opened and aired with a blazing fire at Christmas. Our neighbour used his front room for storing his seed potatoes for chitting!

The other room downstairs which was in constant use was at the rear of the house alongside the kitchen. This was the pantry. None of your tiddly little boxes. This was fully as large as the living room. The brick floor was lower than the rest of the house by two steps and because it was on the south corner of the house its wall and window were shaded by a huge elder bush to keep it cool. In those days there was no refrigerator. The pantry doubled as a dairy. It held a milk separator, a big butter churn and in addition to the shelves of cake tins, kilner jars of bottled fruit and jars of jam there were meat safes, huge earthenware pots and bowls for storing cream, fermenting elderberry wine or making cool ginger drink. Boxes of fruit filled the spaces under the shelves; it was a veritable cornucopia. If we happened to be snowed in for a month there was enough flour and food to see us through.

Along one side was the pitch-lined salting tub which held two big flitches (sides) of bacon, two huge hams and two gammons soaking up the salt before they were rubbed down and hung from hooks in the kitchen and living room ceiling. As portraits they may have been second class but a lot of our visitors admired them and were happy to slice off a piece and take it home.

The weekend had arrived when the big tin tub was unhooked from the shed, brought in and filled with steaming water before the fire. Soaped and scrubbed, towelled off and wrapped in warm flannelette it felt blissful to enjoy the scents as we grabbed a candle and climbed the stairs to bed.

Looking back it is only now that I can understand that Father had to carve his own way through life and by the sweat of his brow and the ache of his muscles built up his farm from a 30-acre rented council smallholding to a 120-acre farm that he could proudly say he had bought and paid for by the time he died. And though he would never let the mask of stoicism slip, he must have felt proud that his life's work was carried on no matter how ineptly by his son.

However the strongest character in this little scene was Mother. From nothing, in often primitive conditions, she made a home, spent a lifetime improving it and worked to make the housekeeping money which embellished the house, supported the business, clothed her, sent me to grammar school and provided the treats which made our life enjoyable.

This was a generation which paved the way through self-sacrifice for the England we know. Their brothers and sisters were well fitted to go as pioneers to Canada or Australia and wrest a living from those hard and unforgiving lands. Life was hard but it made us all the more appreciative of the small mercies – the new boots after the old, the first bicycle, a day at the seaside, the taste of fresh fruit and vegetables newly in season or even the luxury of a fish and chip supper!

Living conditions had been rude and crude in the 1930s. Slowly improvements were effected. Better coal and coke ranges and heaters were put in. One of our bedrooms was converted into a bathroom when we got a hot water system, and a flush toilet saved tripping down the garden. When I installed a petrol-driven generator and lead acid storage batteries we were able to have the house wired and the urban luxury of instant electric light was ours.

The Generator

At night the towns were brightly lit by gas lamps. All houses were connected to the service and streets were lined with the cast-iron standards of gas lamps. At dusk a lamp-lighter cycled round lighting the street lamps.

Out in the countryside darkness reigned. In country houses the lighting was provided by paraffin lamps and candles. The lamp which needed daily filling with smelly oil and a routine trimming of the cloth wick was used in the main living rooms. Smaller oil lamps or a tiny Kelly lamp would burn in other rooms, and candles in a portable candlestick would light us to bed. Most of the house was dim, passageways and corners were dark and frightening to imaginative children. Reading and writing were difficult unless close to the lamp until the appearance of the incandescent mantle which enabled the Aladdin lamp to shine with the brightness of its town gas brother. The stables and barn were lit by oil hurricane lanterns which cast a yellow glow and deep black shadows between the horses.

On the roads early bicycle lamps were fuelled by paraffin; this was soon superseded by the brighter carbide lamp. This was a marvellous invention. The fuel was acetylene gas which was scientifically created by putting dry granules of calcium carbide in a closed metal pot. Drips of water liberated the gas and it forced its way up to the burner behind a protective glass. The great thing about the carbide lamp was the strong white light which would defy the strongest winds that tried to blow it out.

Gradually the towns obtained a supply of electricity carried along mains on huge pylons across country. The villages remained dark and forbidding. As time went by the large houses installed their own new-fangled electricity plants and the brightest place in our village was St Bartholomew's church, where a special engine provided lighting for the vicarage, the church path between the tombstones and the nave of the church itself.

Some of the big farmhouses had had acetylene gas lighting and now changed to electricity. Trying to keep up with the Joneses and enjoy the bright life, we installed a generator with a row of huge lead acid storage batteries in 1950. It was only a 50-volt outfit but it was wonderful. Light at the touch of a switch and anywhere in the house. It was a feather in our cap; electricity before the neighbours. It was a chore going down to the engine-house, to fill the fuel tank and wind away at the 3-horsepower Lister engine until it coughed and reluctantly ran. It became quite a ritual trekking down to start the engine – accompanied by three-year-old Richard who christened it the 'ginser'. We soon became used to the fades and surges inherent in the system and were happy to join the rural

Bedtime, pre-generator days. From left to right: Richard, Elizabeth and Rosemary.

electrification programme later in the fifties, which brought mains supply to most farmsteads in the county.

One of the conditions for connection to the new supply was that the farmer had to guarantee to consume so many pounds worth of electricity. It looked a huge sum at the time but it was peanuts. Within a few years the supply had revolutionised powered equipment on the farm. Before that date mechanical power was supplied by steam engine or even horse gear to drive barn machinery. By the 1930s oil engines were commonplace and soon farm hay elevators and potato graders were powered by small petrol – or diesel – low horsepower engines.

Now we have gone to the other extreme. The whole farmstead, office, computer, barn, machinery, graders, conveyors, cold stores, depend so entirely on electricity that the whole operation grinds to a halt when there is a power cut unless our standby generator can be brought into action. It is typical that if we need to use a piece of equipment in the field away from the yard power points, we take a portable generator out to the field. But like all yeomen we don't take these benefits for granted. The kitchen still holds a stock of candles and a spare cooker ring for emergencies.

6

The Animals

The farm in 1938 consisted of 120 acres of land with two farmyards. At one yard behind the farmhouse was a stable which housed five horses to work the land, a brick and tile barn for storage and a range of fenland outhouses (mainly timber and corrugated iron) surrounding a small crewyard which built up with straw and dung during the winter. The rough buildings housed a couple of sows and their litters, two cows (Lincoln Reds) and their calves. Cut oat sheaves for the horses were held in a galvanised iron chaff house which completed the perimeter of the cattle yard.

Hay and straw were stacked in the stackyard beyond the crewyard within carrying distance for the daily feeding and bedding. The barn held mangolds for cows and horses, cotton seed cake for the cows and bagged feeds from compounders for pigs and poultry or our own barley meal ground at the Glenside mill for the pigs. The poultry were none of the men's business; they were a distaff affair, though some of their feed came out of the wheat sacks in the barn, a sort of quid pro quo for the provision of dinners.

Outside the yard stood a large hand pump which supplied the horse and cattle water from a well and at the corner of the buildings furthest from the stackyard was an iron copper set in brickwork over a fireplace which boiled about 5cwt of small graded out potatoes to eke out the pig meal. These potatoes would boil and steam away under a covering of hessian sacks until tender. It was a treat to go out in the dark in the rosy glow of the firelight and test the tasty little potatoes in their skins.

We had to keep two cows to keep a constant supply of milk for the farm so that while one was in milk the other was got in calf. Since the cows were Lincoln Reds they were put to Horace Chappell's Lincoln Red bull in the village so that the calves were good beef animals to join the other bought-in beef stores. One year while I was still young and enthusiastic I hand fed one of the calves up to baby beef standard and gained a rosette at Spalding Fatstock Show. It is still hanging in the office.

Close contact with animals always carries a certain risk and calls for a pretty basic alertness. Females are not usually considered vicious or dangerous. But all mothers are protective of their young, be they cows or sows or sheep. A common problem with horses was avoiding crushed toes. You had to get very close to the horse to feed it, groom it, plait its tail and mane and put its collar, bridle and tackle on. It was very easy to get an itchy hoof on your toes and the hoof wore an iron shoe and supported a ton of horseflesh. Similar daily risks occurred in the cattle yards where the bullocks did not know their own strength. The chance of getting trodden upon meant that

Father with house cows, Lincoln Reds.

you had to be fairly nimble but the greatest danger was from getting crushed as the animals simply crowded round the tumbrils (cribs) to feed.

The preliminary cleaning of the cribs had alerted the animals to the arrival of feedtime and they all began to look for the grub. With six cribs to fill between thirty bullocks the first sack of feed attracted every hungry mouth and the force of twenty or more strong young lumps of beef weighing over half a ton apiece has to be felt rather than described as they all converge on the first crib. With a hundredweight of feed in a sack on his back the poor garth man cannot do much to push his way through. It always felt as if my ribs were going to crack.

The cows were not quite so hard to approach because they were tied singly but they wore horns and could whip their heads round and deal a sudden blow with the sharp tip: I recall nursing a sore rib for days unable to laugh or even breathe properly. Another danger with the cows was from kicking. Flies made their life miserable and they were constantly jiffling and switching their tails. Some objected strongly to being milked. Lively ones would kick the bucket over or just kick out at the milker. We found that if you were to be kicked it hurt less to be kicked at close quarters before the leg had made a full-length swing. The closer the safer.

One of the funniest episodes took place on the slipe (grass bank at the side of the river) when we went with Grandfather Walter to inspect his bullocks fattening on the grass. They were quite cady (quiet) and allowed us to stroke them and feel their

Father with shire horse, 1925.

flesh. One got very friendly and came up behind grandfather, put its front legs on his shoulders and tried to mount him. It was a bit of a shock to find 12cwt of friendly or amorous beef breathing down his neck.

The milk supplied the house and the farm workers. Surplus milk was separated for cream which then became a domestic item for butter-making, while the separated milk helped fatten the pigs. Surplus beastlings (the first milk or colostrum after calving) was used to make beastling custards, a very rich dessert.

The pigs, cows and calves, like the horses, needed feeding every day, twice a day, come Sunday or Bank Holiday. And the cows needed milking twice a day, morning and night, holidays and harvest time too. We call it doing the chores – and chore it was after a long day lugging heavy sheaves till arms felt like dropping off.

One vivid memory of the pigs recalls a Saturday afternoon when my wife and I proudly looked over the fence at a pen of Large White porkers. They had just been fed with barley meal mixed into an appetising porridge with separated milk. They looked a picture, bright, round and pink, covered in their pretty coat of shiny white hair, standing in clean yellow straw. They grunted and munched at the trough until the largest one, a show specimen, lurched away to the corner of the sty and dropped down dead. A stern reminder that in the midst of life there is death. Or perhaps I had omitted one of Father's old remedies. On Sunday mornings, instead of feeding his pigs, he would toss in a shovelful of slack (the small coal crumbs from the coalshed). This was a sort of corrective medicine like the flowers of sulphur (brimstone and treacle) administered to us and was called 'putting on a streak of lean in the bacon'.

Farm life was a good introduction to the pattern of life and death. The facts of life were an open book and accepted as such. The preparation of food took place in the farm kitchen. This was not just the making of bread or hot cakes when we were cut off from the bakery, it included the preparation of meat both on a large scale at the pig killing and also the mundane business of gutting and skinning rabbits for the pot and plucking and dressing chickens for a Sunday roast. We youngsters soon learned not to be squeamish.

The miracle of birth took place regularly on the farm. The sows produced ten or more pink piglets and unless carefully managed would unthinkingly contrive to lie on a couple of the little squealing critters and crush the new life out of them. Calving a cow was a much longer task and always seemed to take place at night when we were home from school. It was an education to follow the development from the breaking of the water to the appearance of two tiny wet hooves, followed by a head and then a huge body. This was quickly rubbed dry with straw and within minutes young bully boy was tottering to his feet and sucking away. In difficult cases a rope had to be attached to the legs and assistance given. Even the youngsters with eyes popping could be called on to help pull. It always used to fascinate our visitors and I recall Alec Garfoot calling round for a social visit coming out with a lantern to help me deliver an evening calf. It seemed to make him quieter than usual.

Gelding horses and emasculating young bulls were generally done by professionals but the litters of pigs were dealt with by a little old chap from the village. He caught the little pigs and held them tightly between his knees upside down. A quick couple of cuts with his sharp pocket knife and he would throw the product on to the straw with a flourish. The squealing was deafening but it must have been caused by the fear of being caught and pinioned by a strange human because the pigs did not seem to be in pain afterwards. While this was going on the piglets were kept in a separate pen away from the sow who was very agitated by the noise.

We had to absorb the 'birds and the bees' instruction on our own. There were no manuals in the schools, only reading, 'riting and 'rithmetic. These lessons went on any time quite naturally. Father would decide that one of the cows had to be taken to Horace Chappell's Lincoln Red bull on the Glenside where the service took place in the farmyard and afterwards she had to be driven home in full view of everyone! The only mystery to us was how father decided which was the right day. On some farms, if the men were busy harvesting, the girl of the family often took the cow to the bull. The procedure with the boar was different. He did not weigh as much as a bull and was more easily transported in a pig float. He would visit his paramour and stay for a few days.

All this procreation was a serious business and had to be paid for so it was important to get a good calf or litter of pigs. As I recall it was always a solemn business. Recreational sex had not been invented but the barnyard rooster often used to cock his head round with a glint in his eye as he strutted past.

Illness was always near. Vets were expensive and were only called in when absolutely necessary. We had a shelf of homely remedies: Stockholm tar, Coopers cattle medicines, white oils for bad joints and sprained muscles and bottles and bottles of aniseed smelling 'drinks' for colic and gut upsets. We fed a lot of waste

Veterinarian H. Reeks. (Photo courtesy of M.J. Elsden)

potatoes to the cattle and a choke rope hung up in the barn. If a beast got a small potato wedged in its gullet it would blow up with gas until its stomach was very distended. The remedy was either to put the choke rope down its throat to the stomach, then draw out the half-inch cane in the middle of the choke rope to release the gas, or to call the vet and have him release the gas by knife, cutting through the stomach wall. Other jobs which needed the vet's skill were difficult calvings, teeth filing, administration of horse pills (white pills the shape and size of golf balls) and intravenous treatments for foul in the foot in cattle.

In Father's day the vet was a Mr Reeks from Spalding who arrived by motor car in his uniform of knee breeches, shiny black leggings, black jacket and black bowler hat. I did not see a lot of Mr Reeks; schoolboys had to keep out of the way of scientific practitioners though we were allowed to follow the farriers at their shoeing and the pig cutters at their geldings.

We did witness the farewell ceremony. Vets always had a tot of whisky to send them on their way, a libation to the goodwill of the great man or a toast to the recovery of the patient. This traditional cup was taken by all of Mr Reeks' successors. The Spalding vets seemed interested in the more lucrative and less physical small pets business. So our next vet was Mr Emson from Bourne, still in the same uniform and black hard hat. Philip Emson exuded confidence and convinced his farmers that their animals would be bound to recover and only the devil himself could change the process. He was highly thought of and became the official vet for Doncaster race track. Sadly, he was killed in a motor accident returning from a race meeting.

His successor, Mr Jobson, carried on the tradition though without the bowler hat, with practical rubber boots, and maintained the friendly farewell. He was adept at dodging a cow's flying hoof or pitting his strength against a ton of animal muscle as he gave an intravenous treatment for bovine foul of the foot or rasped the teeth of an ageing horse.

The most difficult advice for those vets to give was whether or when to stop treatment. Fees and medicines were expensive and death brought a double loss to the stock owner – the loss and disposal cost of the animal and the practitioner's charges. It really was all creatures great and small and the vet would end his visit to a difficult calving by wrapping a sack round the claws of a fighting cat to complete a neat spaying operation. I think he deserved that little tot for the journey home.

Over the other side of the farm was a cottage and cattle yard. This was a rectangular yard bounded on two sides by a large barn and a cart shed. One other side had a roofed cattle shelter and the last was shaded by huge straw stacks which were used throughout the winter. At one corner stood a stack of rich clover/ryegrass hay. This yard would hold about forty store cattle which were fattened over the winter. Most were kept to heavyweights at two and a half years old. Feed for them was kept in the barn. This would include roots, mangolds, swedes or waste potatoes, rolled oats, dried sugar beet pulp and, richest of all, heavy slabs of linseed and cotton seed cake.

The store cattle were bought from markets at Spalding and Bourne or from further afield, Stamford, Kings Lynn, Northampton or Market Harborough. The purchase of cattle at many markets was a time-consuming business and a lot of store beasts were purchased by cattle dealers who sold them on to the fatteners. A regular supply was shipped from Ireland by dealers like the Purcell brothers who sent train loads of cattle on Saturdays in the autumn for auction in lots of ten or twenty at Spalding Market.

The fat cattle were sent to auctions at Spalding where local butchers and buyers from the large city abattoirs would bid. The cattle were hauled to the market in cattle waggons though I can recall driving bunches of fat cattle from the farm to the market on the hoof. It was a busy job. As outriders on pushbikes we boys had to go ahead and shut all the roadside gates and in town all the garden gates. The side roads had to be blocked off and stragglers chased and brought back to the herd. The cattle drives on the cowboy films were meat and drink to us, we had done it all ourselves.

But all this was hours after Father had drawn his six beasts in readiness. They were carefully selected for the right degree of 'finish'. This meant that they had to be well covered with flesh, strongly muscled at the loin where the best cuts of meat are, and have just the right covering of fat. Not the dry, fatless joints of today, but good, well covered with half an inch of pure fat and finely marbled through the loin in order to produce the superior flavour of good old roast beef. The butchers knew that and the cooks had a hundred uses for beef dripping. This was what Father was looking for as his fingers probed for firmness in the chine area behind the neck and, feeling along the broad back like a table top towards the tail, he would probe the point just ahead of the tail root to test that the sirloin had just enough cover. Then, risking a sideways kick from the object of his caresses, he would run a hand down the inside of the leg to ensure that the flanks were well finished.

As each animal was carefully inspected and passed, it was put into a pen to wait. At last the pen was full of six prime bullocks, each weighing between 12 and 13cwt. A perfectly matched lot of broad-backed Lincoln Reds, coats a gleaming dark red-brown, horns spanning nearly 3 feet, a satisfying picture of health and fecundity. At three years old they would provide a lot of flavoursome plates. Father drilled it into us that the art of producing beef is to buy in the stores at the right price. 'Somebody has to keep them a year for nothing. Don't let it be you.'

Before the Second World War the cattle and horses were sold in New Road, Spalding, and passers-by on all pavements had to be very wary of the streams of liquid manure scenting the air. Sheep were penned in iron-railed cages in the Sheep Market. The auctioneer's man in a fawn slop (smock) rang a big brass bell on the other side of the road against Sheddy Turner's fish shop. The cattle were driven into an iron-fenced pen next to a permanent weighbridge at the entrance to Red Lion Street.

As the beasts were weighed one by one a big clock face over the top registered the weight in hundredweights and quarters. The butchers from home and away sized up the animals on offer, cast a wary eye on the numbers and quality still to come and made their bids. The auctioneer Tom A. White, a prime grade A specimen himself, stood no nonsense and only accepted sensible bids. As each beast was offered he called for a price to be bid and in almost every case the final bid was within a couple of shillings of his opening call. (I omitted to explain that when selling by weight the scale reading is reduced by a 'quarter' – 28lb, to allow for shrinkage.)

Once our cattle were sold, and the auctioneer stated in his preamble that ours were well presented in tiptop condition so that we put our business to him next time, we boys were given sixpence to buy our lunch (one pennyworth of chips and a twopenny piece of fish) from Knipe's fish shop, and then enjoyed a wander round the market stalls before biking home.

All these animals needed grazing for summer feed, and hay and roots for the winter. Over a quarter of the farm was taken up by grass, hay and forage crops. The manure was returned to the soil to nourish the crops. I often ponder the economics of organic farming. On the output of those days we were only able to give a light dressing of farmyard manure to about 15 acres or 12 per cent of the land farmed. Clearly, to organically feed large-scale crops would need vast quantities of organic manure and many acres of crops grown purely for green soiling or ploughing in. The yields would certainly be much lower and prices would have to rise. Ideally large numbers of livestock would need to be reintroduced to our farms. It would not be impossible but the bureaucratic nightmare of licensing, tagging and testing, processing pieces of paper and passporting every single animal is somewhat offputting, and if more farmers switch to meat production in a dead market who is going to pay the wages of our workers and the rents to our landlords?

I grew up on a smallholding before the days of balanced plant fertilisers and before remedies for plagues of locusts or preventatives for murrains and blights were invented. I have spread farmyard manure until my arms and muscles screamed with fatigue – muck had to be handled six times by human effort before being ploughed into the soil. I have seen the heartbreak of tending a crop until the day that aphids

Spalding Cattle Market, 1938. (Photo courtesy of M.J. Elsden)

or beetles took over and the only recourse that the experts could advise was prayer. To 'return to nature' is a wonderful concept, a nostalgic dream. I have been there. I would not wish such a life on my friends any more than I would wish them to undergo surgery in an eighteenth-century operating theatre.

Every animal had its own character and idiosyncrasies. We grew to know them; we gave them names and talked to them but they were always animals. And when the time came for them to go to market or to their next home, well that was why we kept them. There was just a sense of satisfied pride that they had done well and gone away sleek and fat.

The last time we had geese on the farm was 1960. Richard, our eldest, had a wreckling pig as his own. He soon developed organisational skills by delegating the chore of feeding his pig on days when he was late for school in exchange for the reward of a toffee, a penny or brotherly approval. Good training for later life.

Elizabeth had half a dozen bantam chickens and Rosemary, as the youngest, had five young goslings as her pets.

Rosemary took her responsibilities seriously and solicitously fed, watered and nurtured her charges, chattering to them all the while – 'Hello little mateys'. They duly responded with squawks and squabbles and followed her around like faithful dogs. We had heard of goosegirls of years gone by but it was quite a sight to see this little girl of nine years old come home from school and immediately call her geese and take them for a walk up the lane.

It started a couple of generations ago. The geese were part of our family. They only stayed with us for seven or eight months of the year and when they went there was a sigh of relief as happens on the departure of any visitors whose happy welcome gradually cools when the exposure of their true greedy obstreperous strident nature becomes unendurable.

They came in the early days of the summer, little fluffy balls of yellow down already showing ungainly legs, a large beak and beady little eyes. As week-old goslings they had a certain amount of naïve charm. They quickly settled into their quarters, a few wooden coops in a chicken-wire pen to prevent them from running into trouble with the dogs and cats and horses. They were easy to keep happy; constant feeds of poultry meal made into a tasty mash with warm water and a bowl of water to drink. They showed their thanks by gobbling and honking whenever Mother could be seen approaching.

In no time at all those gangly legs lengthened, bodies thickened, a few feathers began to quill on their backs and a fearsome head took shape above a sweeping graceful neck. After three weeks the little pens were crowded so the run was left open and over thirty curious youngsters began to explore.

The farmyard was a place of fascination. There were buildings all round, most with doors closed to keep out marauders and to keep the floor clean. The pens by now were inches deep in mud and paddle – it wouldn't do to mess up the barn and the garage which housed the newly acquired motor car.

With the warm nights of midsummer the goslings began to spend all day and night out of their coops and exercise in the spacious yard. In the middle of the yard beside an apple tree was the farmyard pond: what a joy for paddling and dipping and for dredging out tasty morsels. There was plenty to eat; grass and weeds make good feed for geese and there was no need to stray far away. Except on the days when there was no-one around and then an excursion into the horse paddock or, shame on them, into the vegetable garden, to discover some exciting new flavours.

They continued to grow bigger and heavier and to expand in confidence until they took a proprietary interest in the farmyard. This consisted of chasing intruders with sharp beaks on the attack backed by a concerted menacing hissing. Anyone coming into the farmyard at night would set off a clamour to awaken the dead. We understood exactly how the geese of Rome had alerted the sentries in time to despatch the invaders.

At this stage of their lives they discovered the use of their wings. These powerful limbs looked like the wings of the angels in religious pictures, pure white and strong. The wing of a full-grown goose is powerful enough to injure a man but the domestic goose is so heavy that it finds it difficult to fly. Our geese only managed to lift themselves 7 or 8 feet above the ground but thirty geese taking off on thundering wings to fly across the yard in a flock make a pretty impressive sight.

There is something in a goose's character that makes it insatiably curious and, from that, mischievous. Anything new or unusual has to be investigated. Loose bits have to be chewed and pulled off. Auntie Dorothy, more of an urban than a rural person, cycled down to visit one afternoon and was horrified to find that the geese

Mother with geese, Home Farm, 1941.

had examined her bicycle propped by the wall and diligently unscrewed the metal valves on her wheels!

The season wore on until autumn; Christmas is coming but the geese aren't fat. Father clears one of the sheds and the freedom to roam is curtailed. Penned now in the warm shed on a cosy layer of straw, special feeding begins. Hot boiled potatoes from the farmyard copper mixed with rich barley meal are gobbled up twice a day until a few days before Christmas.

Then the whole farm stops for a day as the plump creatures have their wings pinioned before despatch. Everyone on the farm is pressganged into helping with the plucking. Sitting round the barn with a goose on their knees, everyone is soon covered with white down like snowmen, on their clothes, on their hair, even up their nostrils. At long last the carcasses are taken in to the kitchen to be singed, dressed and trussed. Each is weighed, labelled and set out to cool on the dairy shelves before delivery.

On the day Christmas dinner is a feast. The rich meat of a traditional English goose cannot be bettered. We all pull up our chairs and tuck in – except the Christmas when Rosemary reared the geese. She could only manage to avert her eyes and gingerly taste a sausage.

7

The Rural Economy

Life was a bit primitive in the 1930s but everyone was happy. Our rural economy operated on an almost moneyless system. There was cash, yes, but in such minuscule amounts that it is hard for anyone in the twenty-first century to visualise. Wages were low, 37s a week for a farm worker. A girl had a good situation if she was in domestic service with board and lodging found and a yearly salary of £15.

There was no income support, housing or child benefit, sick pay – and precious little dole or unemployment pay. With so little money floating around, income tax and PAYE were political dreams for the future. For ordinary people taxation meant a charge on beer, tobacco, petrol and such faraway items as death duty, licence fees and stamp duty. Income tax was left for the rich property owners who could carry round golden sovereigns in a canvas bag which would not wear the coins or chafe through their pockets.

For the smallholder income tax was a mysterious charge levied on 'Schedule B' which was related to the annual value of the land. Until the food shortages of the Second World War period farm incomes were so low that little hard cash changed hands and taxation was minimal. Self-help was the order of the day and a week's help with harvesting or thrashing was traded off by working for the neighbours to compensate. The farm office and records depended upon cheque book stubs, a bank statement and a curling heap of receipted bills hung from a nail on a piece of bent wire.

Wage day was a ceremonious occasion. At the end of the week, Saturday noon then, Father would meet all the men in the cart shed and count out their wages from a bag of silver coins. It was Father's duty to meet the weekly wage bill and deposit the cash and cheques for produce and animals sold at Barclays Bank in town. This money was used to pay the rent, the vet's bill and purchase livestock and machinery.

In the farmhouse a different style of finance operated. Mother had responsibility for all inside work. The milk had to be separated twice a day. The cream was saved for churning into butter. What a job that was! In thundery weather or a hot summer the cream would 'go to sleep' in the huge end-over-end wooden churn and take ages to turn into butter. During the heat of the summer buckets of cream had to be lowered into the water cistern overnight to try to bring down the temperature enough to make the butter 'come'.

Another of Mother's duties was to look after the barnyard poultry. Every spring 200 day-old chicks of exotic breeds, White Leghorns and Rhode Island Reds, were purchased. The chicks were nursed along in brooders, fed with high protein purchased meal until they were strong enough to run outside. At about six months the pullets would begin to lay eggs in the nest boxes of the long huts in the chicken pen. Oyster shell grit to help grind the food in the gizzard and make the eggshells was fetched from the merchant in the village. But the buckets of chicken corn, best wheat and tail corn from the barn were provided by the farm. Probably a spot of feminine blackmail – if you want fried eggs and boiled hens to eat you have to supply some corn.

For a few weeks after stooking the henhouses on iron wheels were towed out to the wheatfields where the chickens gleaned the corn and ears left on the field behind the binder. There seemed to be no trouble with foxes and human predators in those days, though it was quite a task finding all the eggs. Many an egg was cracked and swallowed raw by the farmhands before the egg basket came round.

Another domestic task was to secure the meat supply for the farm. There were no refrigerators or deep freezes so in the cool of the autumn and again in the early spring a specially fattened hog pig or a huge fat sow would be killed on the farm. The carcass would be cleaned and scraped outside in the yard. After butchering it was Mother's responsibility to attend to the detail of setting out the joints of meat, preparing the pig's fries, grinding up the meat for sausages, making the pork pies, boiling the brawn and rendering down the lard. All this was done at the same time as keeping a watchful eye on Father who took on the duty of salting the bacon flitches and hams in the big pitch-lined salting tub. There they would lie soaking up the salt until they were dusted off, wrapped in muslin and hung like pictures from hooks in the kitchen ceiling. We lived on pork, sausages, pies and brawn for a month and on salt bacon the rest of the year. My delicate stomach could not cope with the pork after a few weeks. I caught ptomaine poisoning and nearly passed on. After a few weeks I recovered to be a nuisance again but I had lost the sight in my left eye.

Men used to think it was hard work in the fields but it must have been soul-destroying drudgery for the farmers' wives without any mechanical aids in the house at all. In addition to the normal housework and poultry work around the farmyard, the horsemen had to be given board and lodging. The lady of the house carried a very heavy burden and Mother had the help of a maid during this time. Whether Betty was paid out of the farm bank balance or out of the housekeeping money I never found out.

But it was a major part of the rural economy that the chicken money belonged to the farmer's wife to spend as she wished on household expenses. It was as important to choose a good wife as to select the best livestock and horses. The wife was the mainspring of the business from early morning to late at night and could not be exchanged for a new one like a horse that didn't pull its weight.

Her one treat was to go to town on market day, taking her pats of butter, baskets of eggs and any surplus fruit and vegetables from the garden. There she would sit in the Butter Cross at the side of the Corn Exchange and sell her produce in the morning. In the afternoon there was time for a quick look round the shops and a purchase of the tempting goods needed at home, sugar and medicines, buttons and clothes.

It was an economy that worked because we had no other. I have especial reason to be thankful for it. By working her fingers to the bone as she said, my mother provided me with a good start in life, good food, clothes for school but, best of all, a shining example.

8

Schooldays

School was a new world, of classes and slates and slate pencils. Miss Lily May Roe took the infants, Mrs Wiles took the next class introducing exercise books, pens with steel nibs and inkwells, a smattering of writing words and sums. The top class was taught by Johnny Moore, a martinet who had seen it all before and had to teach discipline to strong lads of 13 or 14 who would be at work on the farm after school and could manage a team of horses in the holidays. His persuasion was not honeyed words – more a sharp tongue and a 6-foot long cane. As a precocious youngster I was talking in the back row during his brief absence. Creeping silently behind the curtain which divided our classrooms he whacked me across the backside. A double whammy, one from the cane and one from the wooden bench where my backside overhung to be nipped. I didn't misbehave again.

Here the daily challenge was whips and tops, hoop racing or marbles in season with skipping and hopscotch for the girls. Occasional fist fights added to the excitement. You had to be careful not to pick a fight with anyone with a big brother.

Most of us walked to the school behind the church, about a mile for most of us, past interesting cottages, gardens and pubs, gathering numbers on the way. There was little traffic on the road, a few bicycles and farm horses and carts and occasionally a big hermaphrodite (large waggon with extensions) from Armstrong & Thompson carrying big bags of horse chaff or trusses of hay. On market days Bill Gray, the village carrier, would set off to Spalding about school time, smartly dressed in breeches and leggings, with a trim light horse in the shafts of his cart. We boys used to run behind, out of sight, and hang on the back, until one day I fell down on the gravelled road and cut my bare knees to ribbons. Some kind lady took me in, bathed the blood away, patched me up and set me off to school again.

Johnny Moore did not get a lot of co-operation from parents, nor shining examples, but he did send one or two of his pupils to the High School or the Grammar School each year. I was one of the lucky ones, being given one of the six free governors' places awarded each year. To gain this a troupe of timid youngsters had to attend the Grammar School one Saturday morning, take a written paper and undergo an interview with the headmaster, a tall cadaverous scholar called Lewis (later Cabby) Driver. He asked a few terrifying questions and then set a few simple mental arithmetic posers. He seemed fascinated by the fact that I could add or subtract without pencil and paper, and awarded me a scholarship. I was never any good at mathematics from that day on.

William Gray's carrier cart (West Pinchbeck to Spalding Tuesday, Wednesday, Saturday).
(Photo courtesy of M.J. Elsden)

So the next September father was settled in his new farm in South Fen and I, rigged up in a new blue blazer and a round, crested cap, started at Spalding Grammar School, a new boy in form 3B. New boys were totally green but quickly imitated the old hands at least a year older. It was 4 miles to school now and this meant a cycle ride morning and night, wet or fine; the striking moments were the frosty mornings which nipped bare ears or windy days which always seemed to blow from the direction you were heading.

Over the years we boys from the village built up a camaraderie on wheels, and started long friendships, Cecil Christian, Arnold Edinborough and me. Jimmy Higham from Dunsby Fen followed later. Jimmy was excused morning prayers because he had to travel 8 miles.

Life in the school was totally absorbing and for those days quite broad in scope. It had a wide catchment and prepared many local townsmen's sons to follow in their fathers' business. Activities included organised sport, cricket, rugby, football and swimming, club events, geographical society field trips, debating societies and drama.

We learned discipline – the ultimate sanction being a caning in the headmaster's study – and the pecking order of society through form monitors and school prefects.

Our heroes were the first team at cricket or rugby, and our sole purpose in life was to pass the Cambridge School Certificate exam with exemption from London Matriculation and then on to the Cambridge Higher Certificate.

London matric. demanded a pass with credit in Latin and as we had been joined by a young enthusiastic classics master, Arnold Bottomley, I began a life-long interest in Roman and Greek antiquity. Arnold and his mother taught me a lot about life outside school and through them I became involved in drama and learned to appreciate Shakespeare, Sheridan, Goldsmith and others.

Schooldays came to an end with the usual clutch of certificates, team colours and prefectship and then the challenge came: what to do next?

I had a yearning to go to Cambridge. School hero Joe Bailey had a rugby blue and I sat the entrance exam for an exhibition to St John's. Money was tight at home. I knew what sacrifices mother had made to see me through seven years of grammar school. Unfortunately the Lincolnshire charm didn't impress the dons of St John's but eventually my qualifications earned me a place at Selwyn.

9

Village Characters

To a child in the 1920s all the inhabitants of the village were larger than life characters. All were duly revered for their position of authority, importance in the order of things or merely given deference due to seniority.

The Vicar of St Bartholomew's was such a special figure. The living was in the gift of the Vicar of Pinchbeck, a fact unknown to the people of the west but recently revived in the joint parishes of East and West Pinchbeck.

Father and grandfather talked of past vicars, Wayet and Hoosen, but my first memories were of Parkerson, Grey and Yeomans up to 1946. Parkerson was a lonely soul not really in touch with his bucolic flock, tended by his mother in the cold stone vicarage. He taught me to be a choirboy and server, introduced a few high church touches to his services and endured his exile to the intractable countryside with recourse to creature comforts. It was said that on his leaving for Horsham the vicarage coalhouse was full from top to bottom with empty whisky bottles.

Mr Yeomans was a lively enthusiast who tried to galvanise the village people with sports clubs, concerts and activities of all kinds. His hyperactive style did not include driving skills and he managed to put his car off the high Dozens Bank ramper into the deep ditch at the side without much loss except of pride. He was too good to keep long and at the outbreak of war in 1939 he was soon away to serve as a chaplain in the RAF. The parish was left to the tender care of Capt. Smith of the Church Army for the duration. After the war he returned briefly to marry me and Grace Smith of Monks House, Spalding, before being preferred for a larger parish in the south-west. We were married at St Bartholomew's because not only was it my church but my wife's grandfather had been a churchwarden there for many years, often travelling from his Pode Hole farm in a pony and trap. Later saw the arrival of Francis Cutler who moved on to Crowland Abbey, and Bernard Parsons for a brief stay before Sutton Bridge. It was a poor living and from then on could only support half a parson, shared with either Surfleet parish or Pinchbeck East.

The church also had two outstations: a small schoolroom chapel at Pode Hole and periodic services in the school at Dunsby Fen. The three groups came together for school feast days, Sunday school trips to the seaside and for the rare visitations of the bishop.

The two village churchwardens were elderly pillars of the community with greying hair, dressed in dark suits and brightly shone black boots. They had their own family pews and added dignity to church processions with their rods of office. I recall Alf Gotobed, warden for many years. Before him had been my grandfather Walter

Dobbs and I heard a lot about James Mann, my wife's grandfather. Harold Dring served for several years recently and was followed by our first lady warden, Mrs Alice Cook (née Roe) of Pode Hole.

The most striking churchwarden of recent times was the ebullient Eric M. Cole, who was people's warden at St Bartholomew's, West Pinchbeck, for twenty-six years – an unusually long spell of devoted service. He spent days organising the mowing and tidying of the churchyard, and as mowers and scythe skills dwindled he had the higgledy-piggledy gravestones set in straight lines so that a mechanical mower could take over. He was known to generations of Sunday school children as the man in charge of the annual school feast and organiser of the children's races.

Eric was born in London in 1900 and the family moved to Wales on to a farm, later transferring to Small Drove Lane where they acquired a small farm of 10 acres. Here Eric married Mae Saxton who had been born in America in the emigration surge of the early 1900s. Her parents could not settle there and came home to Marsh Farm, Spalding, from where she married Eric in 1927.

In his youth Eric was a great footballer. He was an enthusiastic right half for Spalding United for many years and had a collection of medals to show for it. The farm was too small to support a family and his energy and determination were harnessed into building up a haulage business. Soon six lorries operated from the farmyard.

In 1939 the war changed village life. Eric was not required for the services so he joined the Auxiliary Fire Service in the civil defence preparations. He was a natural leader with a commanding voice, resounding but slightly nasal, as if his sporting days had left him with a broken nose. With his abounding enthusiasm, Section Leader Cole turned his village unit into an efficient force which won trophies all over the county and even took the regional prize. The unit saw active service during the bombing of Spalding and was called out to a number of aeroplane crashes. The village was proud of the AFS record and trophies. In later years Eric became president of the village British Legion.

In 1950 the nationalisation of road transport put an end to the careers of transport owners and at the age of 50 Eric elected to become a full-time farmer and bulb grower, which he continued until his death at the age of 86. The business at Wyvern House has continued to expand, specialising in flower and vegetable production and packing under the guidance of son Ivor and grandsons James and Andrew.

My last memory of Eric is on a hot summer evening when we laid down our scythes in the churchyard to admire our handiwork. We got round to the subject of last resting places. 'You know, warden', I said, 'I want a spot under that fir tree, beside the vestry door.' 'You shall have it then, boy', he replied. Alas, Eric is now gone – and the fir tree too. My admiration and respect lives on.

The village was well served by Methodist chapels. There was a Nonconformist chapel on the riverside at Boarden Bridge which was strongly supported by the Chappell family until dwindling numbers led to decommissioning and it is now converted to a private house.

Villagers living at the east end of the village supported the chapel in Money Bridge Lane. This was almost the family chapel of the Sneaths. It was built on Sneath land,

Churchwarden Eric Cole with youth club members on a church cleaning project, 1964.

cared for by Sneaths and in my early days Ted Sneath senior bought the public house at Money Bridge in order to close such a wayward distraction. One of the regular worshippers and preachers there was Ernest Smith, farmer, a relative of my wife.

The other chapel was a Primitive Methodist one on Northgate. It had a bigger congregation, fostered the rivalry between church and chapel and only recently closed (1998) – victim of the commuter syndrome where our villages are dormitory sites for a motorised population which commutes for its needs, physical, sporting and spiritual. The services were conducted by visits from a circuit minister and by local laymen, many of whom had the name of Chappell: Harold, Ronald and Maurice.

Everyone had sympathy for Ethel Wiles. She had married during the First World War and her husband did not return from Flanders. Late in life she married Harry Morris, a son of the village who in the strait-laced gossip of the times was reputed to be a bigamist. She outlived him and continued to play the organ regularly at church service as she had done for fifty years. Even from the nursing home in her final years she sent substantial donations for the repair and upkeep of 'her' organ.

The other people of authority in our village were the schoolmaster and teachers. The master was accepted as a man of education outside the school and had to take a leading part in church affairs (it was a church school), organise the fetes and feasts and fairs and even act as an unbiased surveyor in measuring out fields of potatoes and sugar beet in acres or rows for proper payment of the harvesters.

The first headmaster I recall was Johnny Moore, an autocratic taskmaster with a mixed catchment of bright and indolent, cunning or reluctant pupils. Moore was a disciplinarian of the old style. He kept order with a firm voice and failing that, a long cane.

I did not really know Moore's successor Mr Kingston because I left at the same time to start cycling to Spalding Grammar School. The next headmaster was Walter Brumby, a dour north countryman, who I saw regularly as he supported the church in the choir. He married Alice Chatterton, the daughter of Tommy 'Chat', the oldest choir member. Their son John was the same age as our son Richard and often visited the farm.

The school building is now the church hall, a good venue for regular whist drives, dances, concerts and even election meetings.

Like all boys I quickly learned where the village shops were. When we lived in Jockey Drove our grocer was Nancy Riseley at the Northgate corner. She was memorable in that she would deliver our groceries in her open tourer car and knew how to quieten the bairn during the weekly order placing by tossing him a humbug across the counter.

Another shop at the crossroads was kept by the Smith family. At the corner of Leaveslake Drove, Sid Barrows had another small mixed shop and a tall thin daughter Kathleen who joined our Christmas parties. Further on at the Glenside, Len Moon, father of Harold, Mavis and vicar John, ran a grocer's shop just before the Boarden Bridge chapel and near the Bars Bridge; Daddy Patchett had another grocer's – handy for sweets and cigarettes – staffed by a lady reputed to be his niece, though we were not encouraged to enquire too minutely into this relationship.

Our country roads were made for horses. In the fens they tracked along the dry ground, looped round soft boggy places and gave access to the high rampers or joined villages together. Often there was no solid foundation and the lane was two ruts filled with granite chippings set at the width of a cart's wheels with a grassed walkway between for the horse.

Later tarmacadam was widely used to improve the surface. The horses appreciated the new surface because the loads were easier to pull, except in winter when frost nails had to be put in the horseshoes to give a better grip on ice and snow. The horses would be on the road for long periods, half days and full days. After a good feed of hay and chaff in the mornings they tended to leave large amounts of droppings on the roads. To clear up the mess each parish had its roadman equipped with brush and shovel and a two-wheeled barrow painted a dull orange colour embellished with black letters denoting the local authority.

Our roadman was a Mr Patchett, known by all and sundry as 'Daddy'. I never heard his first name. He owned and lived in a small house on the side of the River Glen where the front room, which opened directly on to the footpath, was turned into a small grocery and sweet shop. Takings were meagre and Daddy Patchett supplemented the household income by taking the job of roadman for the local council. He could be seen out all day in all weathers trundling along the roads sweeping and shovelling until the barrow was full, wearing a long raincoat summer and winter.

We never saw where the barrow was emptied. Probably in the fields and hedge bottoms alongside the road. Little did he know the value of his byproduct. Today he could make a useful sideline supplying gardeners and rose fanciers with a good organic fertiliser.

The post office for thirty years was run from a cottage opposite the church and school. Aunty Senior and Poppy Senior conducted the post business, sold a few sweets to the schoolchildren, and when the telephone arrived, the village exchange was located in one room. In those days connections had to go through the village operator who was in a prime position to get the latest news and the choicest gossip. In fact Eric Cole would often break off in mid-conversation to enquire 'That's right, isn't it Poppy?'

We were well served for blacksmiths who shod the horses, laid harrows, sharpened ploughshares and reshod the wooden cart wheels with wide iron tyres. At the Jockey corner there was Harry Deacon; his predecessor had been Louis Mabbot, a fabled character who also preached at the Northgate chapel.

At the other end of the village was the Blacksmiths Row where Nix ruled as the smith. In 1930 he retired and Cyril Carter from Lammings at Surfleet moved in. It was the year that my father moved to Brightman's farm in South Fen. Father and Cyril Carter, starting off together, struck up an empathy which lasted a lifetime. I suppose it still exists because I am an executor for Cyril's estate. He is followed by his son Leslie and grandson Stuart – all in the same mould, clunch (reserved), straight, hardworking and totally opposed to interference from officers, authorities, taxmen and overweening council officials. Who is to say that their ethics and independence are wrong?

Postmistress Poppy Senior, 1914.

The blacksmith's shop was the hub of the village – its information centre. Long before the public houses, the local paper or even the village policeman or vicar heard, Cyril Carter knew who was doing what, and like the oracle could foretell events to come. He knew who was retiring from farming, who was giving up to avoid bankruptcy and why, who was making money or losing it. He knew their private lives and which youngsters would make the grade and which would hasten along the classic journey from clogs to clogs in three generations.

Cyril was a tall, lanky individual, with a sharp thin nose set in a pale white face whose only colour came from an occasional smudge of soot, and piercing grey eyes. He always wore an oily cloth cap which he pushed back from his brow in moments of exasperation. He was a dour character, inhospitable to strangers and to those who sought to impress him or order him about – then five minutes later he would grin and chatter away to his cronies.

He had started his business in hard times. In 1930 his customers got little for their grain, pigs or potatoes. He had a captive clientele. Horses needed shoeing once or more times a year and more often for roadwork. I remember his big leather apron, the sparks flying from the red-hot horseshoes as he shaped them, knocked up the front tab and made the nail holes. The acrid stench of the burning hooves as the shoes were fitted before being quenched in the sizzling cold tub stays in your head for ever. What I marvelled at was the way he could get a ton of horse to perch its hoof on the tripod for trimming or raise it quietly for the red-hot searing of the hoof horn without being kicked to death. His other speciality was in 'sweating' on the rim of a wooden wheel. Every cart, waggon, dray, pony trap or thrashing drum moved on wooden wheels and for road work the iron tyre was needed. The carpenter would prepare the hub, spokes and felloes. Cyril would lay out the wooden parts in position on his wheelwright's plate – a circular flat plate 5 feet across with a hole in the centre for securing the hub. He then heated the iron rim which he had joined in a perfect circle, in a fire of waste wood, until it was red hot. Gripping it with a pair of tongs (with a helper for heavy cart wheels) he would fit the rim over the wooden

Blacksmith Cyril Carter with grandson Stuart. (Photo courtesy of L. Carter)

wheel and if his judgement had been correct, the tyre would cool and contract to fit tightly on the wood, hardly needing the few short nails to keep it in place.

In those years a constant task at the smithy was the beating out of heated plough-shares and horse hoe blades, the repointing and laying (setting level) sets of harrow tines. With the reshafting of hand tools, spades, hoes and forks, and the sale of new blades and grass nails for scythes, the blacksmith had a regular stream of visitors and gossip, especially on wet days.

The farmers also needed machinery repaired, malleable iron fabricated and replacement ploughs, potato spinners and grass mowers. Money was scarce so second- and third-hand was the order of the day. Cyril attended the farm sales and with a shrewd eye for purchasing serviceable equipment soon built up a reputation for supplying sound repaired farm machines. If they did not work he took them back and fixed them. If Father needed a new binder it was good sense to talk it over with the blacksmith and buy from his yard or let the expert check the machine in the sale before one of the pair bought during the auction.

The expert's reputation was prized and carefully worked for. One binder of ours became temperamental and would fail to tie one sheaf in twenty. Cyril walked the length of a 17-chain field studying the action of the knotter. At last a diagnosis – a slight bend in the activator for the bills which held the string – five minutes in the fire and the correct tap with a hammer and bingo, all was well. New technology was added over the years, acetylene welding and hydraulic hose repairs. Our machines only broke down during work and many a lunchtime I have spent eating my jam pasty in the forge while some bent shaft was being straightened or set of shares sharpened.

It was a privilege to be able to go and get a breakage fixed on arrival. Cyril could be a mite selective in his work. Customers who had traded elsewhere would have to wait his convenience and bad payers would wait a long time. He could be very arbitrary and refuse to deal with some characters; from others he demanded cash up front. Yet other customers who were judged worthy would be used as a banking reserve and not receive a bill until the end of the year.

Our accountant wanted all bills in by 1 April each year and it was almost impossible to get the blacksmith's on time. When it did arrive, it was a work of art. Extending over many pages of close ruled lines, it itemised in painstaking longhand every tool, whetstone, nail or nut and bolt for fifty-two weeks of the year, many items of which we had forgotten. A reluctant but necessary chore.

The steady growth of the business over fifty years saw the extension of the premises take in a row of tumbledown cottages, the next-door house, gardens and pub. This business activity brought Cyril into contact with many professional men, auctioneers, valuers, solicitors and accountants, all of whom he accepted as a necessary evil. It was for the very growing army of taxation officers, council men and inspectors that he conjured up his talents of obstruction. As he saw it these parasites did no productive work; they deliberately set out to use their little powers and petty authority to hamper him and he reacted in his gruff way.

Carpenters were thinner on the ground. Next to the blacksmith at the Jockey was Arthur Witherington, who could make a new cart, fit doors, build a chitting house (for sprouting potatoes) or paint your house and measure your fields. He was a quiet man, shortish, about 5 feet 5 inches, slightly built but strong, sandy-haired with a fresh complexion. His most striking characteristic was his quiet voice, slightly hoarse like a cigarette smoker, though I never saw him take tobacco. It was a wise thing for him not to smoke because his workshop was timber built, all his stocks were of various woods and paints and the floor was inches deep in wood shavings and sawdust.

Arthur came from a carpentering family at Gosberton Risegate where his brother Harold carried on the family business. He could and did turn his hand to anything in those days. His workshop usually held a farm cart being repaired and painted. The colour was always red oxide picked out with black furbelows and the owner's name proudly lettered on the side. He could cut and shape the spokes and felloes of the wheels ready for the steel rims of blacksmith Harry Deacon next door. His skills extended to household carpentry and even painting and decorating – though few people then could afford the luxury of paying someone to do their house decorating.

No job was too small. He would even make a couple of hundred chitting trays in good deal timber. In our stock of potato trays I could still find sound Witherington trays after sixty years. When we needed a potato chitting house it was Arthur who came and set out the footings, timbered the structure and glazed it.

There were hidden talents too. The farmers grew sugar beet and potatoes which were singled and harvested by hand. The regular men and casuals were paid by the 'gret', or piecework at so much per acre. It was essential to know how many rows there were in each acre and this is where Arthur came in. He came on to the farm in the evening so as not to disturb the day's work and with his metal chain of 22 yards and a handful of ten iron pins and a wooden square would walk round the field in question and next day produce his independent calculation. As a boy I usually got the job of holding one end of the chain and pulling out the marking pins till I had ten, then we would stop and I would pass them to the man to start over again.

Years later I discovered that the method of field surveying that Arthur used was called triangulation – which was why we carried round the 'square', a round wooden disc on a short spike. In the disc were two saw cuts at right angles for sighting the corner angles and offset sides. Simple but quite accurate for the purpose.

His bills, like all the tradesmen's, were works of art – laboriously dated and itemised, set out in beautiful copperplate. He didn't have a lot of trouble in getting his bills paid up on time. If anyone owed him money he could always get the last laugh. Among his many skills was undertaking. He crafted the most beautiful elm board coffins. Elm was his choice, he told me, because it was the best wood to withstand waterlogging in this fenland country. As an undertaker he did not make a song and dance about his denomination: church or chapel he would bury them all.

Arthur Witherington died in 1956 and his son Gordon carried on the carpentry business. The heavy farm carpentry and cart painting was dropped and Gordon concentrated on house carpentry and home painting and decorating.

Apart from Walter Jacklin on the wrong side of Money Bridge we had to go to Pode Hole to find another nest of craftsmen. Fairbanks the blacksmith, Freir brothers the carpenters and Whitaker the saddler. It is strange how the farrier and the harness maker have come back into fashion. There are now more horses in the village than there were thirty years ago – but lighter animals, for pleasure riding not working.

Our village butchers were T.W. Parsons and Billy Pannell. Their shops and slaughterhouses were close by the Horse & Jockey crossroads. All the work was done on the premises from killing and cutting out to sausage and pie making, and all their animals were bought from local farms or Spalding market. They played a vital part in village life, travelling round farms and cottages killing the winter pigs and dealing in the poultry at Christmas. Council regulations have ended the village abattoir but Bernard Parsons carried on the family tradition for some years and his grandson Andrew has a butchery business at Hawthorn Bank, still serving customers by van until recent food hygiene regulations made it prohibitive to serve from the van at the roadside and he is now only able to deliver meat cut and prepared on the shop premises.

Tobias William Parsons was the village butcher at West Pinchbeck during the period from the First World War until the end of the Second. His early years were spent at Holbeach, where his attendance at Sunday School was marked by the presentation of a Bible in 1894. He trained in the trade of butchery with the London Central Meat Co. (later Baxters) at Wisbech from 1912; he came to West Pinchbeck in about 1917. He married Alice Emily Slator and started a butcher's shop at the Horse & Jockey crossroads. Here he had his own small abattoir where he slaughtered the livestock that he purchased from local markets and farmers; here he cut them up into joints and prepared the sausages, haslets, faggots, bacon and hams and cooked the pork pies and sausage rolls that were on sale in the shop.

Tobias built up a delivery round with his horse and cart during those early years, later changing to a motor van. His wife helped with the cooking and looked after the shop while he was away buying stock and making deliveries.

In those years between the wars life was pretty hard for all villagers. The workers could rarely afford to purchase much 'butcher's meat' but all fattened a pig at the bottom of the garden and all winter Tobias would be busy going out daily to kill a pig for the farmers and cottagers.

I remember him coming down our lane with his van loaded with scalding tub, pig cratch (a flat narrow table about 2½ feet high, with handles at both ends for carrying dead pigs), blocks and pulleys and a wrap of knives, saw, cleaver, steel sharpeners and scruds (metal scrapers for removing hair from pigs' carcasses). He would catch the nominated pig with a lanyard round its nose, walk it across the farmyard, squealing and protesting, to the emptied cart shed where it would be despatched by a quick cut across the jugular with the blood running into a forkful of clean straw. When all was quiet the pig was bathed in the scalding tub full of water from the washhouse copper. Father and butcher scraped off the hair and heaved the carcass over to do the other side.

After the cleaning it was back on to the pig cratch and the men staggered the few yards to the block and pulleys hung from the roof of the shed. For premises without a handy beam a strong bough in the apple tree would do or failing all else a set of tall tripods. Here the disembowelling took place, followed by sawing down the backbone and cutting into joints, hams and sides of bacon.

Butcher Tobias W. Parsons on his delivery cart, 1920s. (Photo courtesy of Mrs Joan Parsons)

This was a spell of furious activity. As fast as the pieces of meat were cut, they were carried into the house where mother ground up the meat for sausages and pork pies, boiled the fat for lard, prepared the pig's fries for us and neighbours and set out the spare rib joints. A delicacy I could never enjoy was brawn, or collared rind as it was called. The cheeks and skin of the head and all sorts of bits and pieces were boiled up and set cold in jelly in every basin we could find to be enjoyed with mustard or packed in sandwiches for a ploughman's lunch. Father was busy meanwhile carrying away the hams and flitches of bacon to salt in the salting tub in the corner of our huge dairy.

To every family in the village the ritual of pig killing was most important. It supplied an abundance of fresh meat for a couple of weeks and ensured salt bacon and ham for the rest of the year.

An inquisitive young imp, I was fascinated by the whole process and was treated to lessons in how it should be done. One little secret T.W. shared with me was the new introduction of the humane killer. It became legally mandatory around this time but the depths of the fens were a long way from London and I was shown how to make a small hole in the pig's forehead with a knife point to simulate the humane killer before the head was carried into the kitchen to become brawn.

After all the activity T.W. would clean his tools, load up the tub and cratch in the van. Before he left, father would bring out the whisky bottle and a half glass of milk. Pouring a stiff tot in the milk to keep out the cold, butcher Parsons would down it and set off up the road in the van while our kitchen steamed up with boiling lard and cooking pies and I was set to turn the sausage machine handle.

Alas, those days can never return. The village slaughterhouses are all closed down because regulations impose exacting conditions and insist on the butcher paying for a vet to be in attendance at every killing day – an expensive imposition for a couple of carcasses.

Drainage is the lifeblood of the fens. If the drains are in good order and working well, crops grow, livestock flourish and everything thrives. The main waterways planned by Vermuiden and Vernatti and the Venturers of Deeping Fen take the excess water to the sea but these are supplemented by a network of large drains maintained by local drainage boards and beyond that by farm ditches and field pipes.

Our local drainage board, the Welland & Deepings, has miles of channels all now running to the huge pumps which keep the water table low and safe. Years ago when there were more cattle in the fens some of the drains ran backward to bring drinking water to grassfields which did not have a supply of mains water. That has now ceased, although the board does still hold water back by headboards and sluices to maintain a water table in very dry gravelly areas.

The system of drains needs constant maintenance. The grass and reed, which can hold up water to a depth of 3 feet over a mile, was once mown (roded) by gangs of expert scythemen. Today machines mow out the watercourses at the rate of miles per day rather than chains.

Fifty years ago the maintenance of the drains was just as important. This was where Jack Mansfield came in. He lived in a council house at Bars Bridge and every day he was out patrolling the drains in the village area. He rode round his patch on a bicycle with fork and shovel. His job was to inspect and make sure the watercourses were clear. Much of the time he had to go on foot because the drains went through the middle of farm land with no road alongside. He had to check that tunnels were clear and clean out any blockages, be they grass or floating wood, and report any slips – places where the banks had fallen in. Jack was a great character, short, wiry and tough. You always felt he was spoiling for a fight.

Sadly in the drive for cost-cutting efficiency Jack was not replaced when he retired so any untoward blockages or slips have to be notified by the farmers alongside the drains, though I believe that Jack's ghost alerts them and shows them where to look.

Our local mill and bakery on Glenside was run by Harold Garfoot. He not only delivered bread and cakes round the village but also supplied the 'balanced rations' for the numerous sties of pigs and flocks of chickens and ground-up farm barley for pig fattening. The sacks were pulled to the top floor of the mill by a chain hoist and the corn ground into meal on the way down. I did not see the mill used with wind-driven sails. By my time it was driven by an oil engine. The Garfoots retired a year or two after the Second World War ended and were followed by Stan Hall.

Jock Westcott, the baker at the mill, was the trumpeter in the local dance band. Most dance nights he would blow his heart out in the school hall till 2 a.m. then go home and set the dough and get the ovens fired up.

At the other end of the village there had been a mill in Small Drove Lane run by a McDonald. It must have closed down when I was a boy and the corn trade and milling for Northgate was centred on Oliver Turner's mill at the end of Northgate.

Dyke Roding, Father, Reg and friend.

The law used to be well represented by a resident village constable, complete with tiny office and lock-up. As a boy I remember PC Parker being held up as a threat for naughty children – he was followed by PC Bell and PC Male. Now we see an occasional uniformed cap passing by in a police car. There is no contact, no human communication. There can be no local knowledge, no feel for the district, no awareness of the arrival of strangers, no presence of authority. We now belong to Neighbourhood Watch but it would feel even better if our parish council levied a rate to settle a retired police officer in the village again.

The other village tradesmen were the 'higglers', and Tom Grooby the thrashing machine owner. Grooby ran five sets and thrashed wheat, oats, barley and seed crops all over the village from harvest until April with steam-driven tackle. One of his sets would go into Bourne Fen at harvest and not come home until spring for its annual repair and paint up. Tom was a law unto himself and woe betide any farmer who wanted his stacks thrashed if he hadn't paid his bill from last year. Tom was followed by his son George who converted to the handier TVO tractors for power – not so picturesque as the steam giants but easier to power up on a winter morning. An important piece of equipment was the cut box which would be towed in for two or three hours of chaff cutting on a Saturday morning. Until the end of the 1950s every farm still had its stable of horses for carting potatoes, beet and corn sheaves, so around the yards were dotted two or three cobs, little round stacks of oats for horse feed.

One or two of the farms had spare time with their tractors and crawlers. Some, such as Albert Roe, would plough land for their neighbours and at the Jockey, Charlie Smith earned a crust or two as a higgler, ploughing and cultivating for various allotment holders. I remember him coming to our farm to lift sugar beet with a new twin-pronged machine that was supposed to do a better job than our old horse ploughs with a lifting share.

Glenside Mill, 2006.

Bobby Gay used to ride to work down the lane from the village on his old sit-up-and-beg bicycle. He came at the civilised hour of 7 a.m. because he joined our farm as he approached retiring age, though in earlier years he had to rise at 5 to feed and groom the horses ready for work. He hadn't been sacked or made redundant but as my Uncle Charles's only farmworker there was no longer sufficient work for everyone on Charlie's small farm after the son left school and came home to work. Bobby simply moved sideways to help us.

He stood about 5 feet 4, with a wizened face, beady eyes and leathery skin. He wore an old cloth cap pulled down over his eyes, collarless shirt, dirty fustian trousers and a waistcoat. Whether he ever changed his waistcoat I never knew, it always looked like the same one with the same holes chafed through at the front and ample pockets for his watch, tobacco and matches. On his feet were hobnailed boots and leather leggings. In his last years these were replaced by leather or canvas gaiters, army issue from the Home Guard. He walked always with a light gait as if on hot bricks – a wide kind of walk, not bow-legged as a jockey, but careful where to place his feet and not to let his toes stay too long in the same place. He may have suffered from corns but we put it down to the constant crushing as the horses stepped on his toes.

Bobby was a real son of the soil, a faithful and loyal servant, and could endure long hours of toil in any weather. He would take his turn with us hoeing thistles in the wheat or weeding potatoes and sugar beet. He taught me the tricks of cut and cover (chop one weed and cover the little ones) and how to keep up with the rest of the gang: 'Walk on where there is nowt.' But his main interest was in showing his skill at controlling the big, powerful, lumbering shire horses that we had. He never did drive a tractor.

His charges towered over his puny frame so that I wondered how he could get the huge collars over their heads, but gear them up he did with saddle or trait chains and off to the field to hobble on his dancing feet up and down for miles every day. He showed me how to yoke a team of two or three to a plough, the tricks of easing the plough a bit shallower in the heavy places, how to lean on the ails or handles to keep the furrow straight as the seam passed through beds of silt and clay, and most important of all how to get a good wide swing at the end of the field so that the plough did not turn over to hit the novice with the ails or allow the harrow pole to turn too sharply and turn over the full set of harrows.

He even taught me to plough 'swing', that is without wheels, simply using the sole of the plough to keep the required depth and using the land slide to control the furrow width. It was an eye-opener when halfway down the field he would judge a horse was ready to stale (urinate). His lips would purse as the horse stopped and Bobby would emit a cascade of short shrill whistles to encourage the rest of the team to use the stop as well, because neither mare nor gelding can stale on the move.

Bobby was full of horse lore to impress us. 'Don't feed much wheat to 'em and if you do cree it [give it wheat], soak it overnight in the sleck tub [metal bowl] and just damp the oat chaff with half a bowlful.' He would rub the horses' legs with oils reeking of turpentine for strained muscles and tendons, dab Stockholm tar on sore places and if colic or bowel trouble threatened, he would pour, down an unwilling throat, drenches of aniseed medicaments from a big beer bottle. He could trim a hoof, dig out a stone from the thrush, tie up a tail with red and yellow ribbons or pad a horse collar with a lady's stocking to stop the collar chafing on raw skin.

Amid all this arcane skill and knowledge he kept his last mystery well hidden. Spanish fly. The very name and a wink and a nod were enough. I imagined that this was the elixir that turned hacks into thoroughbreds and brought jaded animals back to vibrant health, raring to go. And what it would do for you if you gave a small amount to your girlfriend! Alas, he never produced the bottle.

I knew him in the Second World War. Bobby joined the Local Defence Volunteers, soon to be the Home Guard. He had served in the Lincolnshire Regiment in the previous war, so as one of the five experienced ex-soldiers in the West Pinchbeck platoon he was appointed sergeant, though a less military NCO could not be imagined. He had come a long way since the hirings at Holbeach Horse Fair where he told me workers were lined up and hired for the coming year. He married, had two sons and worked for over sixty years with his bike, his dockey (lunch) bag and a bottle of cold tea.

Our last sight of him was in an old people's home at his final Christmas. A little gift of tobacco and whisky, or was it memories, stirred his emotions and tears ran down his face.

Tom Crosby spent his prime in charge of one of Grooby's thrashing sets. The advent of combines saw many of the sets pensioned off. I liked Tom. He was a loner, never married, and while king of his giant steam engine and at home with stacks and corn and machines, he was quite lost in the world of officials and lawyers – a countryman of the old sort.

Our next memorable worker was Stanley Hubbert. He was garth man and labourer. He could claim to be a bank manager because he oversaw the beef cattle on the river bank. He never drove a tractor and was not a horseman but he was the best hand tool man we ever had. He could gap his acre of beet a day or hoe round every plant in a row at a good speed and with potato fork he was used to digging a rood of early potatoes before 3 o'clock while his wife picked them.

Not all of our workers have been tiptop. One, a fellow called Shadbolt, lived in the Slipe cottage. He had a gipsy streak and was not always attending to the task he was given. Some sunny afternoons he would disappear to be found along the river using a four-tined muck fork on a rope as a harpoon to catch the fish. This could not carry on and he was given notice. He refused to move and we had to get a court order for possession, our only recourse to the law. The process caused a bit of excitement because Daddy Patchett came biking down to say that Shadbolt had a gun and was going to shoot me. In the event it all passed off fairly quietly when PC Bell happened to show his face. The gipsies took their revenge in the end. A vacant cottage generally needs a bit of attention before a new tenant moves in. This one was so bad that my wife and I had to go ourselves to clean up the worst of the deliberate fouling of the nest.

Fred and Herbert Strickson were two independent characters who tile drained a lot of our fields by hand and one autumn picked a field of potatoes behind the rooter head plough.

Our rats were kept down by a Mr Beeho from Quadring. Rats in corn stacks did a lot of damage but in the barns they played havoc with the sacks of corn, bags of meal or potatoes and even made nests in bundles of empty bags. Beeho came with a pack of Jack Russell terriers, a tin of cyanide, a bag full of rat bait and a long spoon. He could call the rats out with a squeak or two for the terriers to nip them at the back of the neck. A common sight along the river banks were the lines of moleskins hanging out to dry on the barbed-wire fences. There were no rabbit holes in the banks but it was felt necessary not to tempt fate, and to keep the mole holes to a minimum.

One village character who lived life to the full was Tom Peach – churchman, chorister, farmer, sportsman (he provided the village with its cricket field), clubman at the Constitutional and a thoroughly enjoyable companion on a shoot. He was also saviour of the village during the floods of 1947 when he organised the sand-bagging of the Glen banks as the river waters lapped the trembling top.

We did not have an official village squire, but to all intents and purposes Harold Smith of Willoughby Farm filled the role. He had three farms in the village, a tennis court at his house and was consulted on major village issues. Sadly his son John was killed in a major road accident as he was settling down to the farm after the war. It took the steam out of Harold and the farm eventually passed on to Robert Waugh.

In those days farmers were men of substance and managed their estates. They had workers and a foreman who rode round on a bicycle wearing a bowler hat. One spring Father and I were planting potatoes very early (before March) down Slipe Drove and the three gentry drove down to see whether we were doing it right – Harold Smith, Grandfather Walter Dobbs and neighbour Joe Phillips.

Other noteworthy figures included Ted Sneath who bred and showed Percheron horses at Money Bridge and Sam Freir from Pinchbeck. Sam used to ride down once a week to look his farm over. On his way back he always stopped at the corner by our house to light a huge cigar. As an impressionable schoolboy I watched with wide-open eyes – if that was farming that would be the life for me. Little did I know!

10

The Village Ladies

There was a custom in our village for over a century that with the coming of spring the ladies went out to work on farms. This was before the arrival of PAYE and strict restrictions through employment law. The whole business was informal and privately arranged but was tightly regulated by custom as to rates and conditions of work.

It was traditional for gangs of housewives and unmarried girls to go out in spring planting potatoes and in autumn to pick them for storage. This provided cash for housekeeping, clothes and extra treats independent of the husband's wage, in just the same way that the farmer's wife was expected to manage her domestic economy by managing the poultry and eggs and butter. It was all a vital part of the local economy.

This seasonal work had gone on for generations and most of the workers returned to the same farm year after year. This work extended to the bulb and flower picking in the daffodil and tulip industry where quite large troops of thirty to fifty ladies of all ages in long skirts and aprons and poke bonnets were seen gathering flowers for market from the late 1890s onwards.

A lot of the women helped with weeding the crops, and the introduction of sugar beet in the 1920s brought extra work for them, dividing the small bunches of seedlings down to single plants. This task was often done following their husbands who chopped out the braird (drilled rows of emerging seeds) to sixty or seventy bunches per chain (22 yards).

Haytime and corn harvest were heavier work by comparison with long hours and were mainly left to the men; though during the two wars a lot of women worked on the land and the Women's Land Army was recruited to replace men joining the forces.

One amazing phenomenon was the pea picking. Before the introduction of machines, crops with a short harvest period had to be picked by hand, bagged and sent to market fresh. Here, the village grapevine, helped by a notice in the shop, would produce overnight fifty, a hundred or more pickers of all ages to pick the peas into buckets, baskets or any container to hand.

The grapevine worked both ways. It would bring a huge army one day which could dwindle tomorrow as rumours of a better crop, bigger pods, fewer weeds or twopence a bag more money at the other end of the village enticed workers away. This procedure worked for fresh peas, broad beans, French bush beans, fruit and strawberries. It was an entirely classless system: the schoolmaster's wife worked alongside the farmers' children or the scholars and tramps or artisans, all swarming on bikes to the fields.

We were not politically correct; there was no sex equality. The women could look after themselves. They filled the heavy potato baskets and the men hefted them to empty into the cart.

Alas, those days are gone: the social contact of the small group, the exciting crowds of the big pea fields. The value of the peas and beans has fallen, the cost of the labour has risen, so that it is no longer economic even if it were legal to employ a crowd of people without expensive washrooms, toilets, canteens, first-aid rooms and countless inspectors.

11

Our New Tractor

The farm on which I was born and reared was a smallholding down Starlode Drove. We were there until I was almost 10 years old and I have only faint memories of the fields to be explored, the huge animals and the large garden halved with the next-door neighbour, Harry Branton, who had a large apple tree loaded with sweet codlings for scrumping in sporadic raids.

In 1930 father had the opportunity to rent Brightman's farm in South Fen. This was considerably larger and consisted of a total of 120 acres rented from two landlords, Sir Hugh Welby of Sapperton and the trustees of a Leeds merchant called Butler. In addition a stretch of the Glen bank was available for cattle grazing. This was a good move. It was a bigger farm though the soil was of mixed quality – hungry silt to blue clay, officially classed as 'skirt' soil. I was at school and earned my pocket money by working during the holidays, planting potatoes at Easter, singling beet or tying wheat sheaves behind father's scythe or leading the horse carts at harvest.

All father's profits were ploughed back into the farm, purchasing machinery, buying livestock or improving the buildings. Our first tractor, an iron-wheeled Fordson, arrived in 1938 at a cost of £130. Now we were going to modernise, to mechanise, to come into the twentieth century. Right on time the Fordson arrived. It shone in its coat of bright blue paint set off by garish orange wheels. It was a symbol of the new mechanical era where man was to be in control with power at his finger tips.

Our senior man was Arthur Smith and he was appointed to drive it. He was instructed for an hour and, apart from shouting 'Whoa' a few times to stop it, he gradually learned to manoeuvre the idiosyncratic brute. Arthur left to better himself at Walter Clayton's in Deeping Fen and I had to take over. This meant learning all Henry Ford's little foibles, not the least of which was starting up. The first task was to fill the fuel tank with paraffin (kerosene) with a 2-gallon can and a funnel fitted with a filter to keep chaff and debris out. Water had to be checked. Half a gallon a day could boil away on heavy work. Engine oil was checked daily and the back axle once a week. The latter took heavy treacly oil of 160 viscosity which perhaps accounted for some of the sluggish response. The ritual of starting began with hooking down the clutch pedal and a short prayer that the plates had disengaged.

The actual start was on petrol after draining the carburetter and engaging full choke. The spark was provided by a magneto (a Bosch) which was somewhat

Reg on the new Fordson tractor, 1938.

temperamental. It sometimes needed a tap or kick to make the spring release. A simple retarder slowed the spark for starting, so now we go. A sharp pull-up with the starting handle generates the spark and pulls the mixture into the cylinders. There is an art to starting. With care thumb and fingers are kept on the same side of the handle grip so that if it does start and fails to disengage the hand is not broken. Cough, cough. Again: now a deep-throated roar – no unnecessary silencers! Back out of the cart shed; switch over to TVO and hitch on the plough. This can be a dangerous manoeuvre as the response of the clutch is slow when cold and stop distance could be anywhere between 3 and 5 feet. Many a sports jump champion has trained helping his mate hitch up and learned to leap out of the way.

And so to the field. The main drive wheels were 12-inch steel bands set with spade lugs every few inches to give traction. On soft ground they sank in to bite and gave a fairly smooth ride, but on hard ground every lug produced a bump and on stoned roadways they dug into and churned up the surface so were quickly banned to the verges. The front wheels were of cast iron with a raised rib in the middle of the rim. This helped to turn the front of the tractor on soft ground. On hard ground it doubled the bumps but it was positive steering. Under heavy load the back

Friend Arnold Bottomley on the new Fordson tractor, 1938.

wheels tended to push the front wheels straight forward so that the radius of the turn circle needed a delicate judgement. At times ploughing two furrows of stiff clay would lift the front wheels off the ground – to fall with a spine-jarring bang when the clutch was thrown out.

A comfortable ride was given by a pan seat on a spring steel bar. No rubber cushions, but the chill of the steel seat was softened by a folded hessian potato sack. There were no weatherproof cabs but my thick overcoat proved its worth against wind and rain and in winter a thick sack over the knees provided further protection from the climate.

It was a hard life but I have happy memories of ploughing by the light of the harvest moon following the furrow by feel and sensing the black ditch to turn at the far end. The only light was the glow of the red-hot exhaust pipe sailing along like the devil's staff in the darkness.

It seems a far cry from the powerful juggernauts of today – electronically controlled, air-conditioned, equipped with radio for communication and amusement, operating all manner of add-on machines by power take-off and hydraulic motors. There is even TV monitoring of the operation taking place behind.

There is quite a difference between the old model and the new. The first in 1938 cost £130, the value of about 6 tons of wheat. The modern machine now costs the equivalent of 400 tons but the paint is prettier.

12

Work on the Farm

For the first fifty years of my observing life we grew a mixture of crops. The two main ones recurring every year were wheat and potatoes. During all that time the money made on the wheat crop was so little that in truth the grain crops were simply grown as a space in the rotation to rest the fields until the time came to plant the main (hopefully) cash crop – potatoes. There has always been a lot of hope in farming.

Potatoes have always been a very important crop in south Lincolnshire and until eelworm affected the rotation, the potatoes provided the major part of the income of farmers, paid the wages of workers and supported a huge infrastructure, from railway and lorry transportation to the machinery dealers and distributors serving the changing needs of the crop. An indication of the scale of potato trading is the fact that until the 1960s there was at least one potato merchant based in every village and in some there were two.

The preparation for potatoes was always thorough. A good dressing of ten cartloads per acre of farmyard manure or a dressing of wool shoddy deep ploughed and subsoiled early in autumn to allow winter frosts to weather the furrows was the least treatment for this hungry crop. Some larger farms would grow a crop of red clover, cut it down, apply a coat of farmyard manure, let the aftermath grow through the lot and plough it all in. A wealthy farmer taking new land for potatoes could afford to drill the field with horse beans or tares and when the crop was full grown plough it in, a fine preparation which both enriched the soil and killed the weeds.

At planting time, the women, girls and boys without a regular job would help with the planting. Then every potato was hand-planted down the furrow from a basket or from chitting trays. These workers could plant half an acre each and more per day but picking the potatoes in the autumn was a slower and more laborious task – and backbreaking.

As soon as the corn harvest was finished preparations began for the potato picking to start by 20 September. A small stack of wheat would be thrashed to provide loose straw for wrapping down the potato heaps; in later years the straw was batted in string-tied trusses for easier handling. Potato grave places were marked out, usually alongside a stone roadway or beside the dyke that bordered the council hard road. Not for us the narrow gauge potato railways of the Holbeach Marsh barons. We had to put our potato heaps where the waggons and lorries could be loaded off our shoulders. I would love to see a man today toss a 112lb sack on to a shoulder with a hicking (lifting) stick and dance on a wobbly plank across a 15 foot drain!

Planting potatoes, 1960.

Planting potatoes, 1993.

Filling potato planter, 1993.

The amount of land taken up by potato graves added up to several acres. At least a 4-yard strip of soil had to be left each side of the 9-foot bottom for earthing up with two coats of soil to keep the frost out.

From the middle of September the potato tops had died down and the skins were set. It was considered good business to sell a few acres 'green' straight off the field to finance the rest of the operation.

Before 1939 I recall the pickers were often a gang of 'roadsters', itinerant men of mixed ability from all walks of life, refugees from depressed towns and factories, refugees from domesticity or crime. They dossed down in the potato chitting house on makeshift beds of straw palliasses and sacking and after getting a grub-stake of bread, cheese, eggs and bacon from the farmhouse, soon wheedled a 'sub' on the first day's work to fetch the rations and baccy from the village shop. A very sad story – to this schoolboy it was a first lesson in economics and it made us feel happier with our lot. The Second World War provided most of these men with a uniform or a job. Registration and rationing of food virtually ended such a casual and rootless life.

After 1945 we became dependent on other mobile workers. The Irish had for centuries come over to England to earn money either on constructing the canals, the main drains or the railways and hundreds used to come over every year to help with the harvest. On the farm next to us the same gang came every year. They lived in the 'paddy

Planting potatoes by hand from chitting trays, 1930s.

hut', a purpose built structure of brick or timber and corrugated iron, with a table, a stove and bunk beds. The foreman's wife earned a shilling or two cooking vast quantities of meat, eggs and potatoes and fetching dozens of loaves of bread. She would cook a hot meal for them at night – buckets of potatoes and pans of meat to serve hot that night and cold for midday sandwiches. These men worked long hours; a few visited the pubs on Saturday night but all walked the 4 miles to Spalding to attend mass on Sunday morning.

Their earnings were carefully saved and sent home to the wife and children who, with the help of grandparents, were keeping the small farms in the west of Ireland going until November. These men came in August to clear the grain harvest and stayed until the last of the potatoes were gathered. Our paddies, relatives of the gang next door, came in September just for the potato picking. We began to become more dependent on our autumn gang and the same leaders came year after year. Eventually an empty cottage was made over to them and Mother furnished them with army blankets, pots and pans and cutlery. A few bags of coal and oil lamps were provided. They were a mixed crew of County Mayo natives and Manchester Irish in-laws and all spoke the bewitching brogue, though in later years I suspected that some of them were taking a tax holiday because they would only work for hard cash.

The method used was to plough out six alternate rows of spuds – the front rows, which a gang of six would pick in line abreast. Later the rows left between (the back

Picking potatoes at Home Farm, 1938.

rows) would be ploughed and picked in line abreast again and so on across the field. The gang liked an early start, 7 a.m. or half past, so the horseman had to be out even earlier to get the first six rows ready with his potato plough which was simply a share blade with rod-like forks which spread the row and exposed the potatoes. In later years we used a Hoover, a chain-link elevator digger, which did not leave so many tubers buried but still needed an early start.

For the pickers it was hard, backbreaking work. Each man had one large basket which he filled, carried to the cart and emptied. The cart was kept close behind; the horse was moved on by voice command and a good crew kept the cart in their midst by the stratagem of having the fastest pickers in front of the cart, able to manage the 3-yard walk back to the cart while their novice or elder pickers worked at the side of the cart and simply emptied over the wheels.

Many were the psychological and cunning ploys in the business. An unknown gang would only be allowed to draw part of their wages to deter them from deserting. A brutal foreman needing a gang of six would hire seven in order to sack the worst man. If the gang was short-handed, an Englishman would occasionally offer to make up the numbers. This was a trigger for mayhem. The Irish boys would set a cracking pace and keep it up until they had killed the outsider off. When he got behind the cart so that he could read the number on the tailboard, they would show no mercy and go all the faster. They were long days picking from about seven in the morning until nearly four in the afternoon. Payment was piecework by the acre and in a good day an Irishman could pick half an acre.

The bargain of the price per acre (picking into carts behind the potato plough and twice harrowing) was struck at the beginning and according to the grapevine was the same as the neighbouring gangs. This bargain was binding and held by both parties; the farmer would retain an acre or two of pay to deter deserters but our gang stuck to their word even though the going got tougher. One season I recall was very wet with days and days of lost time and our lads seemed surprised when in mid-November I told them that I could see they were losing out in trying to wait to finish the contract. I would pay them up for what they had done and let them go home.

As country-bred fellows they were tough, could work as no-one else and did not complain about bad conditions brought about by weather – too hot or cold, too wet or dusty. But if they thought that they were getting a bad deal or that a crop like the King Edwards of those days had huge numbers of small potatoes they could complain. Anyone who wants an MBA in labour relations and man management has only to go into the field at 7 a.m. with a breed of six or eight rows of potatoes ploughed out and confront a gang of striking Irishmen!

To keep this gang going at least three, up to five, scotch (two-wheel) carts were needed depending on the distance from field to heap. The man at the grave had to check and fill any ruts in his grave floor, tip the cart and screen out the potatoes. He built an A-shaped heap on a 9-foot base. With care it could be shaped from the cart, leaving just a few screens full to tidy up at the sides. He then had to cover the heap with straw. This was pulled by hand (yaulmed) into welts and laid on like thatch which had to be held in place by spits of soil spaded on. Later we used batts (trussed straw) which was easier to handle and control on a windy day. The graver had to straw his heap up before he went home at night and I have seen one fellow struggling in the dusk 30 yards of heap behind when he had a good crop and a good gang to contend with.

If the potatoes came to the grave very dry at the end of September I have seen neighbour Smith have his graver throw shovelfuls of soil into the heap to keep moisture in and to prevent the potatoes going spongy.

Today machines pick the potatoes and we cannot use them on the stronger soils. This is putting a lot of pressure on the siltier fields because during the war the fenland farms were ordered to grow potatoes once in every three years. Potato cyst eelworm soon built up on the best silt potato fields so that they now need careful handling, long rotations, nematicides and resistant varieties.

One diversion as winter progressed was to take a ride round the district on Sunday afternoon to assess the rate of riddling and to gauge the size of stocks held. Every farmer's graves of potatoes were then in full public view. Particular note was taken of the local Potato Marketing Board member Ray Pick's rate of stock clearance – he was thought to have special information about the likelihood of shortage or surplus.

This interest was spurred by the crucial importance of the potato crop to the county's economy. All the Ps were regarded as risky – pigs, peas and potatoes. The farm income from potatoes was liable to suffer from frost or flood, from blight or eelworm or just plain poor market demand. Our neighbour Len Shotbolt had grown, riddled and put on rail an 8-ton truckload of potatoes for the London market in 1927. He heard nothing for weeks until a phone call came asking him to

Graving potatoes, c. *1940.*

send money to pay to take them to the tip. Cutting his losses he quickly told the impertinent salesman to give them to the Salvation Army.

Things have not changed today. Very heavy investment is needed to grow the crop and the risks remain. Farmers now hope to get a good price for potatoes one year in four or five.

After growing and handling potatoes in all conditions for more years than I care to recall I find there is still a challenge and a fascination in the potato and I still enjoy a well-cooked chip. An English meal is incomplete without potatoes. As my Scottish friend David Sinclair would say, 'There is only one thing better than a potato' – pause – 'and that's two potatoes.'

I first saw beet from 1930 onwards. It had become well established during the 1920s when the British Sugar Corporation set up a network of factories mainly in the eastern side of the country. The corporation was a joint enterprise of private finance and government shareholding. The purpose was twofold: first to create a home-based sugar industry so that in the event of another war the country could manage with less tropical sugar and secondly to provide a guaranteed contracted crop which would offer some stability to farming which was going through a severe depression of low prices and poor markets.

In those days the sugar beet was drilled by a coulter drill in rows 18 inches apart at a rate of 18 pounds of natural seed per acre. This was to ensure adequate plants to

Spinning out potatoes, 1953.

Father picking potatoes at Home Farm, 1945.

the acre and as the natural seed was actually a cluster of seeds in a cortex the braid tended to emerge in clusters and in warm moist conditions it could resemble a row of cress. This thick row was gapped out by the man, using a long hoe, into bunches which were then singled by the man's wife or by gangs of women. Rates of work were high; a man could gap an acre in a long day (with three hours overtime) and his wife could usually single half of that if he had done his work carefully. This work was done by piecework and could not be skimped because the final job was backhoeing three weeks later to trim out any doubles or missed weeds. The aim was to leave 40,000 plants per acre, that is 40 plants per chain.

The farm men could earn their wages at gapping but preferred to leave the stoop work of singling to women and boys. That was my first introduction to work by the sweat of the brow and the ache of the body. We boys, I and the Coolings next door, used to single beet for Mr Alf Gotobed, the churchwarden, for sevenpence for a very long row in the evenings under the eagle eye of the church. We frequently ended on our knees crawling to ease our backs but looking back it was good training for life. No welfare state then. I don't suppose any workers would tackle the job today but when times were hard I remember people used to fall out over who would get the last 'land' or section of beet to do!

It was at this time of year when most of the staff were dragooned by piecework rates that my uncle Charles used to say he could relax, let his men get on with the job and he could concentrate on what needed to be done to the potatoes or the livestock.

Lifting potatoes with a Reekie two-row harvester, 1993.

Grading potatoes, 1993.

Boxing potatoes for store, 1993.

Most farmers knew how many rows it took for an acre in their fields but in a big display of propriety an independent person would be brought in to measure up. This could be a qualified valuer, the schoolmaster or even the local carpenter to demonstrate authenticity. Their allocation of rows set the rates for gapping, singling and harvesting and their calculations were gospel for the potato picking.

Apart from horse-hoeing between the rows and hand-hoeing any weeds in the row, nothing much could be done to fuss the crop up. Early fertilisers for beet were modest dressings of superphosphate and potash with sulphate of ammonia to supply nitrogen. The arrival of nitrochalk was hailed as a breakthrough with the chalk supplying some lime. The material was in pellet form, and so handy to apply and use as a top dressing (by hand) if necessary.

Bugs and beetles, from wireworms to mangold fly, had free rein and once when an early plague of aphids checked the crop by sucking out the sap and introducing virus disease, Frank Walmesley, the local British Sugar Corporation fieldsman, offered sympathy and advised Father to pray for rain. The crop lifted like a field of carrots.

At harvest the beets were loosened by a horse plough which broke the soil at the side of the row and lifted the root. Men then pulled the roots by hand, holding the tops and knocking two roots together to remove the soil. The beet were laid on the ground, two rows into one. This was repeated on the next two rows until eight rows were laid out with a small space between each two pairs which faced inwards. Every 8 or 10 yards a small heap place was cleared and levelled. The roots were then topped by hand and thrown to the heap. It was essential to keep the topping knife well sharpened and under control. In cold weather the blade could slew half an inch sideways and icy fingers would not feel a thing until the blood began to flow.

If the weather was reasonable our men used to like lifting beet because they could earn their regular wage and a bit extra. But one wet autumn, the rains were constant and the mud so cloying that the beet made a sucking sound as it was dragged out. Father and I had to help out. The crop was carted to a heap in the grassfield, covered with rodings (mown grass taken from the dykes) and left for a couple of weeks to dry off, then reloaded to rattle off some more soil and recarted to the yard. We didn't have budget forecasts and interim financial controls in those days but we knew we were losing money. The only question was how much less we would lose if we got some of the crop fit to sell – a sort of inverted rustic economy that bank managers and consultants can't quite follow.

Anyway in those days the beet was loaded on to Dodson's lorries which held about 8 tons and carted to Spalding beet factory. The campaign lasted about a hundred days. The factory always ran over Christmas (our local taste of twenty-four hours a day round-the-clock industry) and closed a day or two into January when there was a heavy crop. Now a standard campaign runs for a hundred and fifty days or more, with the storage and deterioration of roots for two extra months at the farmer's expense.

Many changes have occurred since those carefree days. Natural seed was supplanted by decorticated, clusters were replaced by monogerm; seed coating now presents single seeds as a pellet with its inbuilt fungicide and long-lasting insecticide ready for the precision drill which drills seeds already gapped and singled. Midway in this progress was an experiment with cross-blocking and with mechanical thinning to ease the labour peak at thinning time.

The horse plough lifter and even C.E. Smith's (my father-in-law) steam cultivator lifting six rows at a time were replaced by the windrowing machines – the early complicated Catchpole or the simple Danish Roerslev. Then came the machines which lifted the crop, topped it and elevated it straight into a cart such as the Catchpole Cadet, the Peter Standen machines and finally the six- and twelve-row self-propelled harvesters with a holding tank for a quarter of an acre.

Similar innovations have come in other departments. Soil analysis defines exact fertiliser needs, satellite systems can control the amounts applied to suit the requirements of different parts of the field. Trace elements required can be prescribed and insecticides are available to assist Frank Walmesley's prayer for ladybirds or rain. The probability of an outbreak of virus yellows can be predicted within broad guidelines and early insect attacks can be met by seed coatings.

The hazards and problems of sugar beet growing are just the same as they were sixty years ago. The difference is that the crop is grown at less cost by very few people. Today the crop is drilled to a stand by two men, weeds are controlled by one man on a sprayer and harvesting is done by one man at the rate of 20 acres a day with one or two large carts hauling off the field.

The human effort of the aching back or the blistered hands of sixty or even forty years ago are now contrived by precision machinery and the muscle power is

Lifting sugar beet with a steam cultivator, Monks House Farm, 1921.

replaced by hydraulic rams. Last autumn one man loaded our 3,000 tons of beet with a power loader and elevator.

The future will bring further changes but none so dramatic as those of the last fifty years. There will be a lot of fine-tuning on the systems now used. The British Sugar Corporation is now a totally independent financially motivated company. It will seek to change the contract conditions to its advantage. In this it will have some success. It needs to pay for the quality and purity of the beet it handles even though it is not yet possible to control the juice purity at the farmer's end. Both grower and corporation have to produce sugar at a competitive price that the consumer can afford but if the farmer loses money on a crop, he has to stop growing it. My guess is that the current squeeze on cereal prices will force growers to stick to sugar beet even at poorer returns.

The sugar beet crop is a prime example of the revolution in agricultural technology; it is a contributor to the slimmed-down rural population and is now a puppet in the international political and economic game.

We still make hay on the farm and have done for over seventy years, three generations. It used to be a staple food in winter; seeds hay was made from undersown red clover and ryegrass mixture and was fed to beef bullocks, the house cows and carthorses. Finer meadow hay was used for the calves and nowadays for riding horses.

We have never been tempted to make silage because we had no dairy herd and such succulents as the stock needed could be provided from mangolds, swedes or the many tons of outgrade potatoes. Since only a relatively small amount was

Lifting sugar beet with a twelve-row lifter, 2004.

Lifting sugar beet with a six-row lifter, 1994.

required, about 10 acres of seeds, it was an acceptable weather risk because that amount could be cut in a day and when fit could be carted in a day.

The procedure was to cut hay on a fine day, preferably at the beginning of a fine spell. Friday or Saturday was a good day to cut because that gave the weekend to begin drying and a full week then to cure and cart. We were taught to let the mown hay lie in the swathe for three days. If undisturbed, it will shed a rain shower. Then it should be turned to let wind and sun dry the underside. After a few hours it can be turned again. If the swathes are not too thick and heavy, two can be turned into one ready for the baler. Skill and judgement then come into play. Is it dry enough to bale? Will too much turning knock off the best part of the feed – the leaf? Is it going to rain? With a baler the bales if slightly green can be stacked in heaps in the field to finish curing, always remembering that green hay is better fodder than weathered material. In fact after three rain soakings the feed value of the hay is ruined and the material is only fit to burn or use for bedding!

In the old days we had to turn the hay by hand with two-tine forks and fetch every available pair of hands from the house, wives and children, to help. Then once the hay was half dry it was forked into small heaps which stood well above the ground to catch the wind. Next day the heaps would be turned to dry the undersides and these heaps were next loaded bodily on to the haycarts and waggons.

One man would spear his fork into the heap and lift it on to the cart to the loader. If the heaps were larger, two men would 'pick' the heaps in one movement. With practice the heaps would hold together in one piece; there is nothing worse than trying to fork up odd wisps of hay.

Large farms used a hay sweep to collect the hay when stacking in the field. We needed our haystacks close by the crew yards so we always used horse carts to lead the hay to the yards where an elevator driven by a Lister 1½ hp petrol engine lifted it to the middle of the stack. The trick in building the stack was to keep the middle full so that rain tended to run out of the stack rather than into it.

The stack was allowed to sweat for three or four weeks. Farmers used to kid themselves that it was okay to have a haystack warm up – it improved the quality of poor hay, they said. But putting hay into stack in too green a condition could be very dangerous. It could heat up and take fire. Those long iron rods at the back of the cart shed are stack irons for pushing into haystacks to test the temperature of the middle. If risky hay was being stacked it was possible to draw up sacks of straw as it was being built to make chimneys which could breathe or build in columns of dry dead straw or old hay. Once a haystack began to get hot the only remedy was to turn it and hope to re-stack the hot wet material on the outsides of the stack.

I have seen a haystack go up in flames by spontaneous combustion. It is quite a sight and it is a mistake unlikely to be repeated.

Once the stack had settled we used to cover it with rodings – dyke mowings of reed and coarse grass which was edible as well. These were kept in place by nets or string hangers weighted by bricks and stones.

In winter, sections were cut down the face of the haystack with a big hay knife. It was cut down in neat squares about 3 or 4 feet across – a tidy forkful to carry down the ladder and into the stable or cattle yard.

There was a second cut of clover ready by mid-August. The aftermath of the meadow hay was used for grazing but the clover mixtures grew again to make a lighter hay crop without much ryegrass in it. It could be left to dry on the field for five or six days and then turned and gathered fairly easily.

Hay should have a good nose; it should smell wholesome and have the scent of summer grass. Hay always seems dusty and any that has been wet at any time in the curing can carry a lot of mould spores. This is why apparently good-looking hay is dunked in water before feeding to horses with wheezy lungs.

Self-sufficiency was part of country life and I was introduced to clover as a substitute for tobacco by our waggoner Bobby Gay when we ran out of both baccy and money. I can't really recommend it but it is as good as sugar beet pulp in a clay pipe.

There is something appealing about hay; even the poets feel it, 'Good hay, sweet hay, hath no fellow'.

The highlight of the year was the harvest. This was the culmination of twelve months' work, and the success of the crop and our ability to bring it home in good condition would determine the course of everyone's life for the next year. The master needed a good fruitful harvest and everyone working on the farm needed him to make money to provide their wages and cottages.

Unfortunately in the time between the end of the First World War and the beginning of the Second, agriculture and businesses generally passed through a period of serious depression. For most of that period wheat fetched about 30 shillings per quarter. A quarter of wheat was two railway sacks, each holding 18 stones (2¼cwt) which worked out at just under £7 per ton. Not a lot of money to share out and even in the higher prices of wartime food shortage the return did not rise above £20 per ton. Wheat prices remained at the £20 per ton level until years after the war when inflation took off in the 1970s.

Towards the end of July the green fields of wheat began to turn golden yellow and by August Bank holiday (the first Monday in August) the binders would be hard at work clicking steadily round the fields, laying the standing crop in precise rows of neatly tied sheaves. But first the scythemen had to mow an opening round the dyke sides of the fields so that the teams of horses did not trample the crop. This was skilled work, needing a strong arm to keep up the rhythm and a knack with the whetstone to keep the scythe blade razor sharp. Father was a great mowman. He could go out after tea at 5 o'clock and mow a path right round a 17-acre field before night. I know he did it because it was my job to follow him round with a two-tined gathering rake and draw the swathe of mown straws into sheaves, twist a band of straw and tie the sheaves, leaving them out of the way on the dyke brink.

The mowers and binders could start harvest while there was still sap in the straw because any soft grain would finish ripening on the straw in the stook – unlike the combine harvesters of today which have to wait for the grain moisture to fall to acceptable levels.

At this time of year the horses would be living out in the grass paddocks. So we would give them a feed until lunchtime while the dew dried off the field. Then it was on with collars and bridles and a team of three was hitched to the binder. A team of three was needed to keep a steady pull on the machine through the heat of the day until 8 p.m. There was a break for rest at 4 p.m. when the men stopped for tea. The horses either had a nosebag of oat chaff or a forkful of green clover, and to keep the flies and horse bees from pestering them a hessian fly net was tied over their backs. On Richardson's large farm next door the horses were changed for a fresh team on the binder at 4 o'clock.

In those days before deep ploughing with tractors the fields had only been cultivated by horsepower and I can remember the winding tracks of old creek beds showing through the wheat. No grain would grow in these tracks and in order not to hinder the binder the green rubbish had to be mown by scythe before the binder got to that point.

We boys were cheap labour and the progress of the binder was paramount so we were set to turn the heads of the wheat back in line for the machine wherever the summer storms had laid the stems or twisted them out of line. A steady job, round and round the field until a tiny square remained in the middle. Somehow out of the blue all the boys crowded round with sticks and from nowhere a couple of men with shotguns materialised to take the rabbits bolting from the last few breeds.

The next job was stooking. Six rows of sheaves to a stook row for three men. The best man took the middle pair of sheaves. He spaced the stooks and set four firmly placed sheaves, pushed hard into the stubble, for the centre. If the others could only lean their sheaves alongside, the stook should stand. This was a satisfying task; you could see what you had achieved in a few hours. The drawback was the thistles. The prickles got into hands and fingers and even through rolled-down shirt sleeves. We found out why the rustics were always pictured wearing smocks. The straw wore through our clothes in no time.

The theory was that a well-made stook would keep the grain dry and in good order for a few weeks until stacked. The old hand-tied sheaves were long and made a pointed stook. A good level crop of wheat came off a binder with a bundle of level heads which made a flat-topped stook. This would not shed rain and in a wet harvest I have seen those heads sprouted and grown together so that they have to be bodily pulled apart before carting.

Tradition said that oats in stook had to hear three church bells before being stacked. The reasoning behind this was that oats were notorious for shedding grain so were always cut a little green, and needed time to mature.

At last the grain was all cut and stooked. It was time to get out the carts and four-wheel waggons. Wheels were greased, extending raves (extensions) and corner poles were rigged and carting got under way. Two men set off for the field with the first cart. This was a good place to be in the gang. You worked hard, but you were your own boss in the field; so long as the carts kept moving up to the stackyard no-one hassled you. Your arms might ache fit to drop off before night but there was always the chance of a rest if there was any delay at the stackyard.

Up at the stackyard Father was measuring out the steddles (base area) for the stacks, calculating the width of the thrashing drum and the distance needed for the straw stack. He had to organise the boys from the village who were driving the carts to the field and leading the full loads back to the yard. His aim was to have a 'running' set; that is at least three carts or waggons so that one is being loaded in the field, one unloaded at the

Drilling linseed, 1994.

Drilling wheat, 2003.

Reg loading sheaves, 1943.

stack and an empty cart on the way to the field. The horses pulled back to the yard willing enough. On arrival at the yard they stood at a tumbril full of fresh-mown clover while the cart was unloaded. It was always a mystery how the horses ate long clover with an iron bit in their mouth. They slavered a lot but they managed.

Steadily the stack rose. The art of building a dry corn stack is to keep the middle well full so that the outer sheaves slope downward and rain runs off and, for a firm solid stack, to 'bind' every layer with a well-fitting sheaf just laid to the string band of the layer it is covering.

I learned this lesson the hard way. Harvest brings out all sorts of help and that year Grandfather Walter came out of retirement to see that we did it right. My task was to follow the stacker (Father) round the edge of the stack, feed him a good straight sheaf, put the rough ones in the middle of the stack and lay the binders as we laid the courses round. Every sheaf I laid all day was not quite correct. 'Turn that one over', 'Pull it in a bit', 'Put it out a bit', 'Drop one behind it to keep the heads up'. All day long, hour after hour, an instruction for every sheaf. But I had to admit they did couch down and fit better. I shall never forget Grandfather on top of the stack in his black churchwarden trousers, patient with ancient wisdom, despairing of inept youth.

As the stack grew higher the sheaves grew heavier and our arms ached. Before the days of elevators a man had to stand in the steerhole – a small hole in the side of the

Reg loading sheaves, 1943.

Reg pitching sheaves, 1944.

stack just above the eave. His job was to lift the sheaves from the teemer (man who forked the hay) on the cart up to the binder and stacker. He was equipped with the longest fork and often his slippery foothold was strengthened by a twisted knot of straw secured by thatch pegs. Some farms had a 'monkey', a tall platform which stood at the side of the stack to support the steerhole man.

All this work, long hours in the full force of the sun, because that sun and heat was needed to dry crops, made men tired, hungry and thirsty. Every one had a lunch bag – sandwiches for the mid-day break and bottles of drink, cold tea, oatmeal drink or lemonade. Drink without sugar quenched thirst best but sugar replaced the energy burning away all day.

The best moment came at 4 o'clock when Mother and other wives and their children came down to the field with large cans of tea and baskets of sandwiches and fresh baked hotcakes for a picnic beside a stook while the horses chomped away at their clover. Our fondest memories of harvest are of the sun shining all afternoon and the sheer luxury of those al fresco teas while resting aching muscles.

There were wet days of course. Memory plays tricks and fades them out but I recall travelling with our horses and carts to help Uncle Charlie cart his harvest. For

Straw carting, 2006.

days it rained morn till night and all we could do so far from home was wait in the barn and smoke, talk and play pitch ha'penny till time to go home.

The practice of providing a barrel of beer for the harvest crew had gone by the board in our Methodist village but one or two farmers did contract with key workers to provide them with a fat pig as a reward for the longer hours worked until harvest home.

The binder was the core unit of the harvest. Made by Deering, McCormick or Albion there was one or more on every farm. They lasted for years and then were adapted to be towed by the early tractors. The binder was the most sophisticated machine on the farm and could be kept in working order with a file for knife sharpening, a box of rivets and some spare canvases to pass the wheat straws from the cutter bar across the bed and up to the string tier. The knotter was a very precise instrument; the only remedy if it refused to tie a good knot was to fetch Cyril Carter, the village blacksmith. He would walk alongside, study the action and either perform a magic adjustment or take away the worn bills which grip the string, bend them slightly in the forge and away we would go again.

Before the time of the binder, corn had been cut by the old sail reapers which cut and swept a bundle of grain to one side and dropped it for the tiers and stookers to follow behind. We did see sail reapers still in use but only on crops where the binder could not be used. I have seen them used on seed crops such as mustard seed where the gentler action would not shatter the seed pods and once on a crop of harvest peas where the sweep action of the sails left a clear path for the horses.

Fond memories still linger of sunshine and youth and of beginning to take part in life. And despite the sweat and weariness the sense of achievement on seeing the last cartload come from the field. A job well done.

Time was when a ride through the countryside of the fens would show a series of farmsteads where the buildings housed livestock and the farmyards held a group of corn stacks neatly thatched. These stacks were a visible sign of the farmer's ability and financial status. Big stacks meant good crops and early thrashing denoted a need for early cash.

The building of the stacks was a matter of skill and pride. Father had a small farm so he did not build the big long stacks on a 12-yard steddle which would take two days to thrash and need a lot of stack sheets to cover overnight or during a rainstorm. He preferred a round stack on a 6-yard steddle. This could be thrashed in one winter's day, was easier to keep dry and did not suffer so much from winter rains soaking into a long roof.

The steddle was marked out with thatch pegs in a 6-yard diameter circle and covered with a bed of last year's straw a foot thick. The first load of sheaves was stacked around the middle with the heads up and the butts radiating round – filling the centre of the stack with a solid core which would 'keep the middle up'. Around this core he would start building the walls, always keeping the sheaves sloping outwards and downwards to keep the water out. If a sheaf did not slope outwards one or two had to be laid behind it to give the right pitch. He would work round backwards laying the outer wall and it would be my job to follow him as the 'binder'. This meant that when he had placed the wall sheaves two high I had to 'bind' them by laying a sheaf flat on them as far as the band to bind the stack wall from slipping out.

Cutting corn. Reg is on the binder, Dick Andrew is the tractor driver, c. 1953.

Children Richard and Elizabeth enjoying a ride on the tractor – illegal today!

Cutting corn with a binder, 1950s.

Cutting corn with a binder, 1950s.

Combining wheat, 1996.

These binders had to slope downwards too and often needed one dropped behind to keep the angle right. In practice this meant that I had to pass every other sheaf to Father and lay the other as a binder or in the middle to 'keep the middle up'. Any awkward or mis-tied sheaves also had to go 'in the middle'. This business of 'keeping the middle up' was the crux of the job. A high middle stopped rain running into the stack and meant that supplying the stacker was downhill, a big advantage when sheaves were tossed thick and fast.

Each round of stacking raised the walls a foot. The sides bulged gently outwards. It was not necessary to do much more than place the layers straight up because the pressure of the stackers' boots seemed to press the right amount of swell and the degree of angle had to be watched. In damp or dewy conditions the sheaves did not move much but very dry weather and particularly short square sheaves were liable to push them out further. The weight of the forkman standing on the edge of the stack to take the sheaves from the man 'teeming' the load could also cause slippage. Shiny oat sheaves were notorious for slipping out too far and on many a bright sunny afternoon we had to go down the ladder and hold the unsightly bulge with a stout wooden prop. Not pretty but effective.

So the day progressed, always keeping the 'middle full'. More height meant forking the sheaves higher. The man on the side at about 12 feet high became the 'steerhole man' sweating in his steerhole, tossing sheaves above his head. His feet would be set on a firm hold of thatch pegs driven in under his boots or he would be

Combine with corn cart, 1996.

perched on the 'monkey'. This was an arm-wrenching job in a good crop; the sheaves were harpooned at the band and the weight of the heads hung down and got heavier as the stack got higher.

The steerhole was usually at the widest point of the stack and roofing began by filling in the middle again and building a small stack in the centre. From here on we needed an extra forkman to toss the sheaves to me. I passed them down to Father so that they landed across his thigh with the butts forward. He then laid them, each one sloping butt downward, gradually tapering the courses inward and always keeping the head ends up.

Finish the course, fill the middle and start round again. And again until only a tiny pinnacle remained. These stacks would keep dry all winter with only a few thatch pegs to stop the gales blowing the sheaves up and a couple of forkfuls of dyke rodings to keep the rain off the top sheaves. These stacks did not need thatching and could be thrashed in a day, saving a night-time covering with stack sheets. Later came 30-foot long elevators drawn by Lister engines to take the place of the steerhole man. In all our time on the corn stacks the well-laid sheaves felt safe to walk on even though our boots sank in deeply.

There was rivalry between the field gang and the stack yard men. The quicker the cart was loaded the longer the rest before the next one. The faster we at the yard emptied the load the longer our drink time. At the bottom of the stack we at the yard had the advantage but as we got up to the roof the men in the field were laughing.

At last the day came when I built my first stack. It stood firm and high. The best stack in the yard.

Lincolnshire is the home of the thatcher. After harvest the hard-won stacks of wheat were thatched to keep them dry during the winter's rains. The equipment was simple – a long ladder which would reach from the ground to the top of the stack, usually a 32-stabber (stave) ladder, some balls of twine wound on to pegs and some bundles of thatch pegs (called thack pegs in our village).

A pair of stout thack pegs hinged with plaited twine at one end and a twine loop at the other completed the tools. Herbert Strickson, the thatcher, came from the village when all the farm staff were busy ploughing, drilling winter cereals, harvesting potatoes and all the busy autumn work for the changeover to winter stockyarding. But the thatcher needed a server – someone to prepare his straw and carry it to him on the precarious side of the stack roof. This was where I came in as the learner. I was 'spare man' and was drafted in.

A heap of straw was dumped at the side of that stackyard and well wetted with buckets of water from the horse tank. The straw was of a good length – cut with a binder while young and thrashed by a beater drum which did not smash it too much. The water took the brittleness from it and allowed it to be drawn from the side of the heap into 'welts' about 3 feet long.

The job of drawing from the heap was called 'yorming'. The trick was to draw it and pull it neat and straight side by side to make a 'welt' about 18 inches to 2 feet across and about 3 inches thick. The welt was then laid across one of the carrying sticks and back to yorm some more. The next welt was laid across the first so that the thatcher could separate each welt on its own to lay it on the stack roof. About half a dozen welts crisscrossed over the stick and the other stick would be brought over and looped to the one on the ground. The whole bundle could be hoisted on my back and carried up the ladder to Herbert who needed it to be placed just so, halfway up the roof.

By now he had got his thack pegs ready, a line of them stretching from the eave to the roof with about 3 inches left showing. By the side of each peg was a ball of twine on its little peg. He started at the eave giving the thatch a bit of overhang to shoot the rain out from the stack and progressed methodically upwards, carefully overlapping the last layer until he reached the top. Each line of pegs was added to about every 2 feet across the roof and the twine was brought across and tied to the new peg. The rows were neatly carried up the roof at intervals of about 2 feet.

And so on, row after row, sweating in the sun or swearing at the breeze, because wind and loose straw make fools of men. At last the rows of thatch and pegs join up and the ladder can be taken away as the twine is tied off on the first row of pegs.

Taking a pride in the work, a pair of sheep-shearing clippers trims a neat edge along the bottom. This is purely cosmetic because the untrimmed longer edges carry the rain out further away from the stack.

One job which went on intermittently throughout the winter was thrashing. This took a lot of organising. A cartload of 'steam hards' had to be fetched from the coal yard at North Drove station to coal up the boiler of the steam engine and bundles of large thick canvas railway sacks had to be got into stock for the corn.

The day had to be agreed with the machine owner and extra men hired to keep the steam engine supplied with water and to feed the drum and cope with the sacks of grain and huge volumes of straw. Weather rarely stopped the operation unless it rained all day or blew such a gale that loose straw simply blew away for miles. Most larger farms had a sheltered stackyard with trees planted on the windward side.

The engine driver would pull down the lane towing his thrashing drum and a train of associated machinery, chaff cutter and elevator. With great skill these huge lumbering monsters with massive iron wheels 6 feet high and 18 inches wide in the tread, would make stately progress down the narrow lanes and turn into the restricted gateways to the stackyard. If possible this was done the evening before so that the tricky manoeuvre of setting up could be done in readiness. In the morning the driver, in blue engineer's overalls, would bike down and fire up to get a head of steam for 7 a.m. If he was working far out in the fens he would have to start at 5 in the morning and during the light nights he would not damp down the fire until 8 p.m., a long day.

His was a privileged position. He was in charge of the tackle. Men had to carry out his bidding, even the farmer; and in summer when the thrashing season was over his job was assured – in the yard cleaning and mending the equipment. The other men were not so lucky. There were a number of men in the village who owed allegiance to no master; they were independent and self-reliant. They offered their help to farmers with a work problem in summer or had an acre or two of allotment of their own and in winter they filled in their time with a bit of hollow (tile) draining or followed the drum for a few days thrashing.

The engine driver usually sorted out how many hands the farmer had and arranged to bring the necessary extras from his regulars. A full crew would total eleven or twelve men so a day's thrashing could be hard work but at the same time an interesting social occasion. Everyone had a favourite task – usually seeking a clean one on the corn stack or stacking the straw. The dusty job of bagging the chaff or clearing out the pult hole (waste straw, small broken pieces from the drum) ended up going to the timid and no-one seemed to want the corn carrier's extra wage of twopence an hour for weighing the 18-stone sacks of wheat and carrying them on his back up a ladder on to a waggon or across to the barn. There was a knack to handling these big weights and I've noticed that often the best carriers were quite small men. I can testify that it is a hard job and the coarse railroad sacks were quite capable of chafing shoulders raw.

With everyone in place down to the water boy, who was given a yoke and two buckets to fetch water from the pump to slake the engine's thirst, it was time to uncover the corn stack. This meant taking off the thatch covering from the roof. In later years we dispensed with the thatch and merely covered the peak of the stack with reedy dyke rodings well pegged down and draped with string or net hangers. We had found that a dry stack remained dry if the sheaves sloped outwards and down. No amount of thatch could keep a roof dry if the sheaves did not shoot the water out and away.

A wet roof meant trouble. The sieves and screens were liable to clog and the wheat was swollen so that the sacks would not hold the correct weight and tie up at the neck. If this happened the first fifteen or twenty sacks would be marked with a wisp of straw tied at the neck. I never did find out what happened to them. Probably mixed in with the bulk because specifications were not very tight and grain was accepted at 16 per cent moisture and even 18 per cent for some grists.

If the rain had been kept out of the roofs, sheaves would dry and keep in good condition for months. In very wet harvests, in desperation, some fields were carted wet with water running out of the bottom of the cart I am told. I have pulled some of these wet stacks apart six months later and they had dried through completely. The sheaves had gone flat like boards, took a lot of pulling apart and were so full of mould and dust that we all looked like coal miners.

The engine driver and his mate took it in turns to feed the drum for a couple of hours. A boy alongside picked up a sheaf and passed it to the feeder, neatly cutting the string at the knot as he dropped the sheaf in the feeder's arms. The feeder stood in a small well just at the drum mouth. There was no guard rail, it would have been in the way. There were low fence boards to stop anyone falling off over the side of the drum deck but it was only a step from a gruesome mauling inside the machine.

At the other end of the machine the dust and chaff and straw came pouring out. Most of the straw was needed for cattle yards. The nearby corn stacks were positioned about 5 yards from the site of the straw stack so that a wooden straw elevator delivered the straw on to the stack. Stacking was a good job. Straw without the grain was light and manageable unless there was a strong wind blowing and then it became one of the tortures of hell.

Later thrashings would find the corn stacks further from the cattleyard and to reach the straw stack site Tom Grooby's machines were fitted with an ingenious device of a pole and wheel on the straw stack with a driven wheel at the drum which propelled a long loop of steel wire on which bundles of straw could be conveyed up to the middle of the straw stack. The bundles were held by a single piece of rope with a hook fastener which unlatched when it hit the wheel on the pole.

The huge bundles were smoothly roped by Ernie Gray, a tall bony individual who was as thin as the rake he used to control the flow of straw. Ernie could make his 'bottles' of straw, chat to the nearest neighbour, twist the huge bundle towards the wire, pull the wire under the hook, and instinctively without looking tap the wire with his rake to drop the returning rope or pult net without breaking sweat. He made it look easy until you tried it.

When the time came to raise the pole and lengthen the wire, the corn stack men had to down forks and man the three guy ropes while the pole was being lifted. Shouts rang out, 'Slack off at the tree', 'Pull up behind', 'Fasten off in the fields', until all was to the engine driver's satisfaction. Team work and camaraderie, a thing that is rare in these sophisticated mechanical days and I miss it.

As the stack got lower we found that it had provided a dry home, warm nests and food for rats. The men on the stack were quite adept at knocking them down with their forks as they scuttled away. All the farm terriers were excitedly running round at the foot of the stack. They looked, jumped, nipped smartly at the back of the neck, a quick toss over the shoulder and off for the next. It didn't seem possible that there could be so many rats. We had to get them all; mustn't let them get into the barn and chew holes in all those new railway sacks.

Tom Grooby's thrashing set, c. 1930.

Tom Grooby's thrashing set, 1954.

During the war the War Ags (War Agricultural Executive Committee) brought in a regulation which required fine mesh wire netting to be put up round the base of the stacks. This was a good idea and any rat which did not run away under the thrasher was likely to be caught. Tom Crosby, the driver, was the only man I knew who could put his hand down a rat hole, pull out the rat by his tail and hit it on his boot.

After thrashing, the grain was stacked two sacks high in the barn until sold. The sacks held 18 stone of wheat and bore the legend LNER or M&GN stamped in foot-high letters, as they were hired from the railway station.

Once the stacks were gone the rats and mice had no home. Those that escaped death as they ran from the steddle liked to sneak into the barn, and it was common to find, when the wheat had been stored a week or two, nests of them breeding behind and in the sacks. They did not eat a lot of grain but they played havoc with the sacks, chewing holes in all directions. At loading time my apprentice job was to stitch up the big rents with a sack needle and twine and to plug the smaller holes with a tightly twisted plug of hay.

We could take the top sack straight on our backs to load the lorries. The bottom ones were wound up to shoulder height on a winding barrow. The sacks were carried to the lorry bed and set on it. If the lorry was too high the carriers had a block of wood to climb to make it easier to set the sack down. The top sacks, the riders, had to be carried up a ladder. I guess we were men in those days though the barley sacks only weighed 2cwt and oats were a doddle at 12 stone!

In the early days the loading was into trucks at North Drove station. The sacks were loaded on to our long four-wheel horse waggon. Most of us could get the top sacks on our back to carry to the waggon. The bottom ones had to be raised by hicking barrow or by winding up on a sack winder to get the height for carrying. A two-horse team pulled the waggonload 2½ miles to the station at North Drove and came back for another load after getting a ticket for the returned full sacks.

On one of my early trips to the station with Bobby Gay something upset Prince, the big black shaft horse, on the main road. He began kicking and almost took the waggon off the road. He smashed the front board of the waggon before Bobby could get him calmed and under control. I took refuge back in the waggon and begged Bobby not to tell Father when we got home. He didn't and it is a mystery to this day how the front panel of the waggon with the owner's name and farm proudly painted got repaired.

On Tuesdays Father would go to Spalding market with a few linen sample bags in his pockets to show them round the buyers in the Corn Exchange. As well as local buyers, millers and maltsters would send their agents from Lincoln, Burton, Lynn and as far afield as Hull and Leicester. The sample bag was opened, examined, smelt for taint and a few grains spilt into the hand to check for split grain, thin kernels and weed seeds. If a bargain was struck the quantity was noted and the bag went into the buyer's suitcase for a check on delivery.

Father sold a lot of consignments to Mr Perry of Henry Watters, Leicester. A shake of the hand and both men could rely on delivery up to sample and payment thirty days after delivery. Local buyers also bought for themselves or to send to other mills. Birch's, Plowman's, Tindall's all had their men visiting farms, and our local miller and baker Harold Garfoot regularly came down. The drill was the same. He would walk along the rows of sacks, punching hard now and again. If the sack yielded, the corn was dry. If it stood firm against the punch it was damp, no messing with moisture meters and Hagberg tests in those days. Smell also counted – good grain smelled sweet, trouble smelled musty.

We used to grow a field of barley and the sample from good fenland used to look plump and bright. The merchants all used to examine it carefully, look wise and knowledgeable, 'It cuts a bit steely, Mr Dobbs, it'll have to go for pig feed'. When it was loaded out the lorry driver said he was taking it to Darley Dale at Burton upon Trent, a well-known brewery. 'My, my', thought Father, 'they must keep a lot of pigs at Darley Dale.'

A few amusing things occur in village life, usually unlooked for. A neighbour was always a bit late paying his thrashing bill. One year in revenge the machine owner would not come in with the thrasher until all the other customers had finished. It was almost time to cut the next year's crop and by some stroke of fortune there was a shortage of malting barley. The next crop from southern counties was not yet ready and the shortage became acute. This fenland high nitrogen barley was offered round the markets and bidder vied against bidder. This odd lot made the top price of the year, a record malting bid.

It does not always pay to be first or to settle your bills too quickly!

A few years after the war we still stuck to the traditional ways even though it got harder to find men to tackle the dirty, sweaty work and to find men able and willing to physically deal with the corn sacks.

One autumn we were trying to thrash and truss some wheat straw ready to cover the potato harvest. Men were in short supply; it was a hot day. My job was on the corn stack forking the sheaves to George Grooby, the new machine owner, who was feeding and cutting his own bands.

As the stack got lower the struggle to lift the sheaves got harder. I must have been trying hard and had put two sheaves up when George only wanted one. He taught me a lesson. He deliberately picked up the lower sheaf so that the upper one slipped off down on to my head. He taught me a lesson all right, that the day of hard labour and unhelpfulness had to end.

Next harvest we had our first combine.

Up for an early breakfast. Tom Thrower had been in the stable since 5.30 feeding the teams in readiness. The stalls were warm and steamy as the huge horses munched steadily through their chopped oat sheaves.

Gearing up proved a difficult operation. First the collar so heavy to lift over the horse's head. It had to be put on upside down to get the big bony head through the wider part at the bottom and then twisted round and settled back on the massive shoulders with the hames (two curved pieces of iron or wood forming part of the horse's collar) up above the neck, pulling the mane out so that it didn't chafe. The trait chains next with the broad back band snug and the large links joined to the collar hooks. The bridle came last over the hemp halter. Neither Jolly nor Blossom would open their teeth to the bit so it was a struggle. Eventually the huge mouths opened and

Ploughing with a team of three, 1944.

with the bit at the back of the teeth the blinkers and head strap could be pushed over the top of the head by standing on tiptoe. Pull out the forelock and fasten the strap below the jaws and we were ready. The check chain went over the right-hand hame and the line was slipped through the bridle rings and tied to the right-hand ring before the neatly coiled line was hung on a hame ready for the journey down to the field.

This business had to be done just so on the line horse because we drove our horses on a single line, not like the farmers in the north of Lincolnshire who had a line on each side of the bridle.

At work the line horse responded to a steady pull to come to the left with the instruction 'come here' or 'cobeer' and to a few smart jerks on the line to go right with the words 'Heet up'.

At the field hitching up was easy. They had all done it many times. The trait chains were looped on the heel trees and Jolly's false line was tied to Blossom's trait so that he was held back a foot or so to keep her in the lead.

Ready for off. With my line wrapped round my left fist I stood between the plough ails (handles) and off we went. 'Whoa!' As they turned in, the plough keeled over and knocked me to the ground. Tom was there to set me right and show me how to lean on the ails to stop the plough digging in until we were at the furrow. From then on it was learn as you go. A touch on the left ail to cut a narrower furrow on the bend or a shove on the right one to make the plough bite a wider furrow in the siltier spots where a bend appeared the other way. Where the team struggled to pull through a clay hole the plough depth could be eased out by pressing both ails down so that the point did not bite quite so deeply but this was frowned on.

Reversible ploughing, 1993.

At the far end of the field the plough had to be eased out by pressing the ails down and running the breast on its side on the landslide along the headland to the other side of the rig before setting off back again.

And so on all day with the scent of fresh-turned soil and the sight of earthworms wriggling in the mould. Soon a flock of seagulls followed the plough, snatching a juicy meal.

During those long hours you become aware of the varying textures of the soil, the clouds and the weather and the quiet swish of the plough as it cut and turned. Everything becomes an event, the hare loping across the field on his mystic pilgrimage, the pheasant proudly strutting his domain, the visit from Father to check the progress and quality of work. At eleven we stop on the headland for a bait (lunch), a bacon sandwich and a flask of tea. We don't stop long. It is chill out in the breeze, sitting on the frame of an iron plough, and we have got to cover an acre in the day.

So we continue, rain or shine, stitching our pattern across the field. Tom shows me the skills; how to finish off a neat furrow, how to set up marker wads to open and close a rig but doesn't let me try any of these things. It is as much as I can do to keep my furrow middling straight.

At three o'clock we get back to the headland and unhitch. There is no way those horses will turn back for another round. They know the time. We jump on the horses' backs and ride back to the stable. Water, feed, ungear and curry comb and brush out the sweat marks. Chaff to cut, corn to cree for the sleck bowl, mangolds to clean, bedding to get in and hay for suppering up.

A good hot tea with plenty of meat and fried potatoes and apple pie. Afterwards Tom plays his cornet in the chaff house while I listen to the champing teeth at the manger. Proud to be one of the men.

13

The Roadsters

A few villagers helped out at spring planting and harvest and before the war there were large numbers of 'roadsters' – men without homes or jobs who would drop in for a few weeks casual work, dossing in the sheds. They were a sad lot, down and outs, down on their luck, refugees from another world which no longer accepted them, cared for them or even acknowledged their existence.

When they were 'set on', Father would go to the farmhouse, get them a mug of tea and a big doorstep sandwich, lathered with dripping and bulging with bacon and cheese. Each newcomer was shown where to get large hessian beet pulp bags to make himself a straw palliasse and bed covering on a makeshift frame in the glasshouse – a warm building for sprouting seed potatoes with the luxury of a central stove which would burn wood or coal and coke. Here they would live for the month or two that the root harvest lasted.

As a schoolboy I was fascinated by these visitors and whenever I could break away from the parental eye I would slip over to the glasshouse to learn more of these alien creatures from the outside world. They were a motley crew. Almost all, to me, old men, with their secrets behind them. No one asked of their origins. All were members of the brotherhood of the road. Fugitives from the law perhaps. Rebels from the constrictions of family life. Unspoken victims of wifely harassment or infidelity, ex-soldiers, one an ex-schoolmaster. All the dregs of society, lost characters who were joined together in a forlorn effort to keep their freedom and eke out a precarious living by earning a few pounds before moving on. Their living was rough, the work grinding and debasing.

They had nothing and expected little. A dry shelter, a meal on arrival, a 'sub' of a few shillings to purchase bread, tea and condensed milk from the village shop. After a couple of days' work a further advance of silver would allow them to purchase bacon, eggs and sausages which they would fry over an open fire on tin lids used as frying pans. Later they would have enough money to buy meat to put strength into their wiry bodies.

To my innocent eyes they were fascinating, mysterious. To Father they were part of the hard economy of the time. They came, did the tasks put before them without question and accepted their lot. Father had to manage them as he would his stable of horses. He provided shelter and an income, carefully rationed sums of money which kept them sustained with food and tobacco (a black plug, pared into slivers for smoking or quids for chewing) but not enough money for booze except on

Saturday night and enough of the wage held back to deter them from absconding till the end of the work.

Some would show me how to fry their supper, some would talk of a past life. Digger had travelled Australia and had tantalising tales of his journey along the Great Barrier Reef to set my imagination alight. Brum was no raconteur but showed a professional dexterity with a pack of cards and the three-card trick. All were identified solely by a town of supposed origin – no names. Yet none ventured an explanation of why they had severed the links with family and friends, why they had opted out of duties and past responsibilities. These were the colourful characters who contributed to my education in worldly wisdom in those autumn months.

Before Christmas they all drew the remainder of their wages, burned their beds and plodded up the lane with a better pair of boots or a warm coat to find their winter quarters.

They and their colleagues turned up regularly every September until the war started. In 1940 they were not good recruiting material for the services but factories in war production demanded workers. Identity cards and ration books required a more specific name than Taffy and Jock and a more permanent abode than the open road.

As a social phenomenon they were unique and short-lived. To me, they never seemed to grumble or complain; they didn't fight or fall out among themselves and I never saw them the worse for wear from beer. Their pleasures were small ones. A warm fire on a cold night, the comfort of a strong pipe of baccy, an old tune on a mouth organ, even a read of the *News of the World*. Now they have disappeared from the face of the earth, their freedom a hostage to the welfare state. The evocative names they carried are now ciphers, a set of lifeless numbers given them by grey civil servants.

They were a glimpse of history; to a country boy they were the other face of urban industry. Where did they march to every December? I would love to know.

14

Leisure

The hours of work on the farms were long and the toil was hard and backbreaking. To hear my father one would get the impression that villagers simply lived to work and sleep. Certainly the days were long – officially fifty-two hours a week in summer before overtime and in my youth at least half a day every Saturday. There was far more livestock. Every farm had its herd of cows or beef cattle and pigs. Then horses had pride of place and were the power unit for the holding. All these animals had to be fed and tended seven days a week – by hand with no transponder feeders or mechanical byre-cleaning devices. There could, it seemed, be no time for boredom or play.

And yet social life in the village was more active than today. There was a lot of spare time to be filled. In summer sixteen hours of daylight could be enjoyed and in winter sixteen hours of darkness limited the amount of farmwork that could be done except for an hour or two in the stable or cow byre by lantern light.

Many events were organised by the church and village groups and it would be a very curmudgeonly farmer who would not allow his family and employees to take part. In the 1920s and '30s village concerts and magic lantern shows took place in winter in the schoolroom. Visiting concert parties were appreciated and whist drives and dances were regular events and raised funds for charities or village needs. The regular MC for the whist drives was Harold Chappell and the trumpet player in the village dance band was Jock Westcott, who can hardly have gone to bed some nights because his job as baker at Garfoot's mill caused him to get to work at 3 in the morning.

The alternative night life was at the pub. The pub was always frowned on in our family but the village was well endowed with a public house or an ale house every furlong or less so that there was not far to walk. Most of these had a landlord who had a daytime job and left his wife to look after the pub during the day, or the inn had a field or two attached to help eke out a living from a few crops.

Sadly the living got smaller; most of the ale houses closed and we now have one licensed premises only and this relies on a good proportion of catering.

The parson and the schoolmaster were involved in every aspect of village life. The school had the only room large enough for concerts or dances and the school was a church school so the co-operation of these two was very important and nothing could take place without their approval.

The Mothers' Union (church) and later the Women's Institute (largely chapel) were very active in organising monthly meetings of a social, entertaining and

Mothers' Union tea parties, c. 1950.

West Pinchbeck concert party, c. 1950.

educational mixture; they also supported good works and organised outings. Earlier the church had been active in organising a young men's association, the church lads, a football team and boy scouts.

What I recall most vividly is the school feasts of the 1920s and '30s. To us youngsters this was a long-looked-for day. The event took place in Mr Robinson's grassfield, the one behind the church school. The festivities started with a short service in the church followed by a procession led by the Spalding Town Silver Band along to Bars Bridge, along the riverside, through Mr Robinson's farmyard and back across the grassfield where the field events began. The band played during the afternoon and evening. Barwicks brought along swingboats, a roundabout and a device where a sharp mallet blow sent a runner up a tower to ring a bell at the top.

Field sports, throwing the bean bags, skittles, bowling for a pig, drew competitors from far afield and a great attraction was the pillow fight on the greasy pole. Here two contestants met on a well-greased pole over a ditch full of water. The trick was to knock the opponent off into the water without getting dislodged yourself. Easier said than done and the prize was a pig!

For the youngsters, the scholars of the Sunday school, there were races, flat, sack and obstacle, competitions for fancy dress, the best decorated bicycle and a huge tea with jellies and cakes. After the children were taken home to bed the whole thing finished with a dance in the school hall.

For this occasion the three sections of the church parish joined together, a contingent from Pode Hole and as a really memorable highlight the party from the

Terence Parsons, Henry Chapman and girls on the Sunday School Feast obstacle course, c. 1954. (Photo courtesy of J. Brumby)

outpost at Dunsby Fen used to travel up in a couple of decorated waggons drawn by beribboned horses.

My father used to tell me of the village football team, of the hair-raising antics at election time and stories of the macho contests between the young bloods who would for sheer devilment challenge one another to hoist a couple of 4-stone weights above their heads or carry a sack of wheat of 2¼cwt the furthest up the lane. It sounds like hollow rustic bravado, but the same sparks took a pride in their work and would ride round on their bikes on Sunday mornings to see whose drilling was straightest.

Winter brought different pastimes. There were a series of hard frosty winters and farm work came to a standstill. Father and his cronies used to skate on their pattens along the drains and once skated along the Forty Foot drain all the way from Jockey Drove to Boston. In those days before the New Cut (Coronation Channel) Cowbit Wash used to flood every winter. The fenland skating championships were held there and the giants of the day (the Slators, Pridgeons and Culys) would sweep along on their long Norwegian blades. For ordinary races the prizes were simple – a joint of beef, a leg of mutton – and very acceptable because in those times a lack of work brought a loss of pay.

Village primary schoolchildren dancing at Sunday School Feast. (Photo courtesy of J. Brumby)

West Pinchbeck Football Team, 1922. Back row, left to right: T.W. Abrams, H.E. Chappell, C. Smith, C. Alexander. Middle row: G. Peacock, O. Garwell, F. Chatterton. Front row: G. Cope, F. Strickson, F. Coupland, J. Sharpe, S. Broughton.

West Pinchbeck Football Team, 1947. Back row, left to right: H.E. Chappell, K. Brooks, P. Summerfield, R. Harker, K. Wilson, N. Wand, G. Watson, W. Rigby, H. Houghton, W. Wand, D. Houghton. Front row: M.K. Chappell, J. Chappell, H. Walpole, E. Rye, J. Christian.

West Pinchbeck Cricket Team, winners of the Cricket Shield, 1937.

I enjoyed a few days on the Wash, biking to Lock's Mill, strapping a pair of skates on and skating as far as Cowbit lighthouse (the church steeple). Just skating on Cowbit Wash was an adventure. Travelling along you had to be alert to dodge the fence posts and barbed wire strands that poked above the ice and with crowds of several hundred people on the ice at any one time there was a real danger of the ice cracking and letting everyone through. In truth there was little danger of suffering anything worse than wet feet because the water was rarely more than 18 inches deep but of course we used to spread rumours of people dropping through into the drainage ditches of deeper water and disappearing. The only mementoes for most of us were a crop of bruises and a few chilblains round the ears.

Spalding town was 5 miles away from the village and was the centre of civilisation, business and shopping. The farmers relied on the market to sell their cattle and pigs and on the Corn Exchange to sell their grain, buy their fertiliser and to get the latest information on the potato trade on the street between the Red Lion or the White Hart and the Corn Exchange. There always seemed to be more potato merchants on the street than in the exchange.

It was a hive of activity and a farmer could make or lose more money on the day's trading than he could earn in a week labouring back on the farm. It was an eye-opener for us boys too, going to market, herding six or eight great fat bullocks along the streets riding as cowboys on our bikes.

The market place on Tuesdays was full of stalls selling everything from buttons to boots, cloth of all descriptions, cheeses and vegetables, haberdashery and tools. There was even a mobile scissor grinder and knife sharpener. During the afternoon Sam Kingston, one of the auctioneers, held a sale 'on the stones', a paved area round the drinking fountain at the west end of the market place where a miscellany of farm equipment, tools, sheets, chains and similar treasures was on offer. Here I bought my second motor car, a majestic Humber 6-cylinder machine which was a smooth powerful runner but the devil to start on a hand crank.

On Saturdays there was no cattle market or corn exchange but the variety of stalls were open for business until late at night and provided an exciting sight, lit as they were by blazing flares. When everyone had their wages burning a hole in their pockets, the sweet stall, where the owner was making toffee and pulling sticks of rock and humbugs before your eyes, made an irresistible attraction.

The journey to the bright lights and fun on Saturday nights was by bicycle. The economics were simple. Sixpence for the night. Twopence to park the bike safely in a lock-up next to Knipe's fish shop on New Road. Fourpence was left to spend at will. A penn'orth of chips and threepence to splash out on the stalls for a bag of toffee and gobstoppers or a fish and chip supper at threepence and a walk round – the permutations were all carefully calculated.

By the 1930s the smaller farmers had to keep up with the Joneses and everyone who was anyone began to buy a motor car. Father started with a second-hand Austin, and changed to a smart Hillman Minx in 1938 – an ex-police car one year old.

The car made visits to town easier. The cycle journey on Saturday night became a car ride to enjoy the pernicious luxuries of the cinema, at first the Prince's in Westlode Street and then the luxurious Regent in the Sheepmarket, where to gain entry one had to pass the bemedalled, magenta-uniformed Sergeant Lorraine of the waxed moustache. I knew him secretly of course as the PT instructor at the Grammar School.

Other great occasions were the fairs and the circus. I was too young to remember the hiring of farm men at the fairs though Bobby Gay, our horsekeeper, told me of being hired for the coming year at Holbeach horse fair and of meeting his wife there. The farm year started on Lady Day, 6 April, and that was the big flitting day. Horse and waggon would be sent to collect the new man, his tools and his furniture with his wife and family riding on top of the load, riding to fresh fields and pastures new.

The arrival of the circus introduced us to strange animals, sequinned girl acrobats and jolly clowns. All great fun. But since we were farmers the highlight of the summer was the county Agricultural Show with its prime cattle, sheep and pigs, gleaming horses glittering with brasses and rows upon rows of agricultural machinery and tents full of beer and sandwiches. The lords of the day were the smartly clad stewards with their bowler hats and walking sticks, who made the whole show run smoothly.

Somewhere in the mists of schoolboy memory are the visits to Smithfield Show. An early morning train ride to London, a lunch at our accustomed time of 11 a.m. when we enjoyed the standing meal of the Metropolis at that hour – breakfast of fried egg, sausage and bacon. Then down into the mysterious underground to the Show where we saw the prize fatstock and the machinery of the future among our peers. Later we visited the West End where we must have stood out like clodhoppers in the Lyons Corner House. A foggy grope round strange streets brought us to the Palladium where the warmth tried to induce sleep which the variety acts vainly combated until train again and home.

Life had its lighter moments. Music played a bigger part than today when everyone is tone drunk from being deafened by transistors. Boys used to whistle a lot; it was the thing to whistle the latest tune. Almost everyone played an instrument, piano or violin. Even if you could not afford a piano, there were always plenty of mouth organs or even the Jews harp that I learned to play in the stable. Tom Thrower, our horseman, was an accomplished cornet player and the village had its own dance band.

Perhaps the one introduction that most changed our life was the coming of the wireless. At a stroke the world came into our home. I had dabbled with the mysteries of science and red-hot technology by making an early crystal set and listening to the faint magic of music coming over the air waves and progressed through my schooldays to build more sophisticated sets with real rectifyer valves and amplifying units. Through being so close to the marvels in the house I did not realise how the life of every household and cottage was changing. We had newspapers for national and local news but now the world news was in our living rooms as it was happening. It was possible to sit in one's own front room and listen to the cup final or a world heavyweight boxing match and know the result before the newspaper office.

The early receivers (now called steam radio) were cumbersome things. They had to be connected to a 30-foot long aerial hung from a pole in the garden. We had no electricity supply so the Cossor or Bush wireless had to be powered by a large dry-cell battery of high voltage (about 120 volts) and the power for the valves came from a wet (lead/acid) accumulator. This had to be charged every week at the local garage so everyone had two – one in use and one under charge.

The wireless set always sat on a shelf next to Father's chair so that he could decide whether we heard the 9 o'clock news only or one of the splendid programmes from London. And what a selection there was; all the latest music and tunes from the bands of Jack Payne and Henry Hall. Budding ballroom dancers could practise steps later to Victor Sylvester with his 'quick, quick, slow'. Greatly liked were the variety shows where artistes like Gracie Fields, George Robey and Rob Wilton could perform in our own living room. The countryside was no longer so isolated; everyone listened to the solemn declaration of war over the radio in September 1939 and a steady diet of *ITMA* with Tommy Handley did much to keep everybody's spirits up in the wartime years.

Looking back there was a lot of pleasure and enjoyment in simple things. People had to create more of their own amusement. As young men and women we were taught the virtues of work, of respect for our elders and those in authority and made to work for the pennies and sixpences that we wanted to spend. We had nothing but our youth and were happy.

15

Transport

Before 1914 all local transport was horse drawn. The motor vehicle was a rarity. Heavy carthorses pulled carts, waggons and drays to deliver goods, beer, coal and forage from the town or the railway station, and personal transportation was by riding horse, pony and trap or carrier's cart. Failing that, the bicycle was gaining in popularity and there was always shanks's pony – on foot. The main roads were metalled but the side lanes and droves were made of 3-inch granite stones in the wheel ruts with grass between. I remember cycling with Mother down Slipe Drove to visit Uncle Fred and Aunt Nellie, tumbling off the bike and cutting my bare knees badly.

Travel was not easy in those early days and many farm workers only left the village once a year to go to the hiring fairs. A lot of journeys were by shanks's pony; as recently as 1950 the family of Ashers at John Smith's Pickworth Drove farm would walk the 6 miles to Bourne church every Sunday. Cycling to work and play was the rule for ordinary folk. We used to visit relatives on our bicycles or by riding pillion on Mother's large machine. On the main roads travel was smooth and easy but on the byroads often the metal was only 3-inch granite chips.

The people of substance, established farmers and business people, travelled by pony and trap. My wife's grandfather James Mann travelled from his farm at Pode Hole as churchwarden to St Bartholomew's, West Pinchbeck, with his family in an open dog cart.

All goods were transported by horses pulling iron-tyred carts, waggons and drays. The farm waggons were a common sight and small packages were delivered to the village by Bill Gray's carrier's cart. The breweries maintained their own fleets of horse drays for delivering barrels and crates of bottled beer to the pubs. Provender merchants Armstrong & Thompson had teams and waggons with wide raves for carrying bulky loads of hay and chaff for feeding the many town-based horses.

The main backbone of national transport was the railway system which served most villages. The distribution of goods and collection to and from the railway station was entirely by horse. The rail system had superseded canal and water transport. Before my time small coaster ships used to bring coal, fish and other cargoes up the Welland to Spalding and a lot of the wheat, barley and oats which were not ground at the village mill were transported by barge. The Forty Foot drain was used to barge grain to Boston.

The farmsteads and barns were built on the banks of the Forty Foot so that the sacks could be carried from the barn down to the barges. At our Guthram farm the old brick cottage, once occupied by a Jobey Swan, and barn were at the far end of the farm away from the road on the edge of the Forty Foot. There are only traces of brick left now and a sunken well.

The internal combustion engine changed the dominance of the horse and railway. Early lorries had the advantage of once handling only and for local delivery work demonstrated their ability to travel further than horses. The great rail strike of 1926 created a golden opportunity for the motor lorry to get a toehold in the intercity trade. With the advantage of door-to-door pick-up and delivery, road traffic began to develop to the virtual exclusion of rail goods traffic today.

The same internal combustion engine changed business and social life in the countryside. There were few motor cars before 1914 but after that war professional men and landowners began to purchase the new status symbol. The doctor, the vet, the auctioneer all paid their business visits by motor car, and social visits were possible further afield. For ordinary people the village bus made excursions to the seaside possible (Skegness or Mablethorpe were annual Sunday school trips) and a local service to Spalding market made the journey easier.

Soon after the war ended Walter Dance of Cowbit Drove started a bus service from the village to Spalding on market days, Tuesday and Saturday. His route was along Northgate and through East Pinchbeck. This bus was called Bluebell and was chain driven. Mother and I used to make the journey on Tuesdays. It was an adventure, picking up passengers along the Northgate road to Pinchbeck, over the Pinchbeck railway approach, the highest hill in the county of Holland, and when the bus had a poorly day the men passengers had to get out and push it up to the top.

A year or two later Horace Nightingale started his fleet of Reliance coaches offering a daily timetable from Gosberton Risegate, West Pinchbeck, past his depot at Pode Hole on to Spalding to cater for shop and office workers as well as shoppers. It brought a big change in leisure outings because people could not only visit shops and cinemas in town but could also organise trips to Skegness or Hunstanton and the Sunday school outing became an annual feature.

After the war firms began to use motor lorries for delivering goods. Cliff Dodson started operating lorries from the end council house in Jockey Drove; he delivered farm produce to town markets and sugar beet to Spalding beet factory. He soon had several lorries and as our smallholding was next door he often sent a 'waggon' to load sugar beet after dark by lantern light. It was all forks and strong-arm stuff in those days – no mechanical loaders. Cliff and his family moved to a bigger site at Pode Hole just before the Second World War and prospered until the Labour government took him over under Nationalisation.

More motor cars appeared on the roads. In the 1920s the merchants and businessmen, the solicitors, doctors, vets and big farmers were driving around in cars and even small farmers began to get an Austin or a Morris to go to market.

16

Wartime in the Village

On Sunday 3 September 1939 at 11 o'clock in the morning the Prime Minister, Neville Chamberlain, broadcast over the wireless that the country was now at war with Germany. We had been on alert for some time. Emergency services for air raid precautions had been recruited, mainly from ex-service personnel from the First World War. These ARP wardens were put on a war footing and began to serve night duty at the village post on a roster basis. Father and many of his cronies began their duties after a full day's work. The fire service was boosted by recruiting an Auxiliary Fire Service unit in the larger villages. These chaps were very enthusiastically led by Eric Cole, the churchwarden and ex-footballer. He trained a team of younger villagers who were inspired by his enthusiasm and took prizes for fire drill and efficiency.

I was still a schoolboy, having left Spalding Grammar School in the summer and not yet enrolled in Cambridge University. I had been given a place at Selwyn College to read classics but with the whole world about to be turned upside down, after a lot of heart-searching, the quiet cloisters of learning did not seem quite the right place to be. All my friends were enrolling in the forces; Bill Watson in the Navy, Ray Holland in the paratroops and from our village Jimmy Higham in the Air Force and Arnold Edinborough in the Army. Cecil Christian from Barclays Bank joined the Royal Artillery, later to be captured by the Japanese at Singapore. John Smith from Monks House was in the Royal Corps of Signals and his brother Bernard was in America training to be air crew in the RAF. It seemed right to leave my studies and do something practical towards the war effort until my call-up came.

There was plenty of physical effort required on the farm and shortly after the declaration of war the War Office decided to muster local able-bodied (and not so able-bodied) men for defence duties under the stirring label of Local Defence Volunteers. These were quickly organised into units covering the whole country with duties of local defence, observation, road-block checking and generally relieving the army of such minor duties and helping the police look out for enemy agents, spies and fifth columnists. It sounds a bit far-fetched today but there was widespread apprehension!

The framework was quickly established. The 2nd Holland Battalion covered the area of Spalding, including Donington, Holbeach and Crowland under Lt-Col Robert Cooke MC. 'B' Company of this battalion covered the villages of Pinchbeck, West Pinchbeck, Surfleet and Gosberton. No. 4 Platoon was the village of West Pinchbeck.

Wanting to do our bit those of us not in the ARP, the AFS or other government services met at the school field. We were a motley crowd, ex-servicemen, farm

Reg, 1940.

workers, young men waiting to enter the forces, like Walter Dring, a local farmer later killed in the Air Force.

Past war service quickly provided our NCOs; Privates Shields, Houghton, Gay and Martin were made up to sergeants and Bill Rigby, our only MM (military medal for gallantry), was a ready-made platoon sergeant. The Company Sergeant Major, a publican named Alexander from Pinchbeck, had a magnificent bearing and a voice to make the dullest yokel jump to it. We were a bit short of officer material so we had an ex-machine gun corps officer sent down from HQ.

Officers of B Company 2nd Battalion, Home Guard, 1944. Back row, left to right: W. Elderkin, J. Rowbottom, A. Elderkin, S. Hill, J. Garner, Lt Hamilton, J. Carter, H. Casswell, L. Marriott. Front row: E. Bain, Lt Garrett, Major Tom Casswell, Capt E.W. Needs, Capt J. Cadas (MO), H. Taylor, R.C. Dobbs.

At first there were no weapons except a few shotguns and no uniforms except a few armbands. Gradually, over a couple of years, this army began to take shape. Uniforms appeared in stages, even regulation gas masks and steel helmets. Weapons too came in bits and pieces – Canadian Ross rifles 300-calibre thick with grease, Browning automatic repeating rifles, a few ex-aircraft Lewis machine guns, one Boyes .5 anti-tank rifle to deter the Tiger tanks, a few Mills hand grenades and wonder of wonders (it was still Capone and Cagney time) a real American Thompson sub-machine gun. Later came quickly manufactured, almost blacksmith-

Home Guard B Company 'Stand Down' Parade.

made, Sten guns and Blacker & Northover projectors. I was always a bit doubtful about the accuracy and efficacy of the projectors but the most certain and devastating weapon we had was the sticky bomb. This would have made life very uncomfortable for the crew of any tank, no matter how large. The only snag was that it had to be placed on the tank by hand with a smack to make it stick – a true contact weapon and a good medal winner.

School friend Ray Holland, now a promising lieutenant in the Parachute Regiment, advised me to join the Intelligence Corps. Sadly he was blown up in North Africa, but he had overestimated me. I volunteered and was turned away even from the infantry because of my eyesight.

So I settled down to become a food provider and a part-time Home Guardsman. The training was not too difficult; just two spells a week of two to three hours and a few trips to the firing ranges or night exercises. Discipline was exacting – a follow-through of the service training of the First World War and a certain camaraderie and authority existed. Yet throughout, the daytime calling would show through and NCOs were perhaps tolerated rather than respected. Our platoon officer Lt Bill Gostick, coming from outside our community, was accepted to have appointed authority. His Machine Gun Corps survival, tall bearing and swagger stick carried off the part completely.

At a later stage since the platoon mustered a hundred men (company strength in the army), the high command decided that Lt Gostick needed a second in command.

Pte R.C. Dobbs, Home Guard, 1941.

After casting about for likely candidates, I was selected, probably on keenness alone – as Bill G. said later, he did not believe in keeping a dog and barking himself.

Anyway, after a spell of probation, a few days of training in a live ammunition battle school in Surrey, I was gazetted in Part II orders as a second lieutenant in the service of king and country. Quite a jump from bare arm private and difficult for a callow youth to perform in front of the experienced ex-soldiers and mature farmers and tradesmen in the platoon. Such were the exigencies of wartime, because everyone had his own problems to deal with, I became accepted and took over a lot of the training. When the OC was promoted sideways to Battalion HQ I took over the defence of the parish and gained a couple of junior officers: 2/Lt Les Marriott, a farmer, and 2/Lt Edgar Bain, a drainage engineer. Our training continued; concrete blockhouses and ammunition stores arrived, and a local schoolmaster, Corporal Easton, took over the stores and the form filling.

We had various premises. Training was in the village school and in the school yard; our guard duty point was the Bars Bridge with a guard hut nearby for the men on standby 10 p.m. to 6 a.m. (two hours on and four off). What happened to the bridge before 10 was anybody's business but that was company orders and all our men had a full-time job. We used various headquarters, usually beer houses. The front parlour of the Bridge Inn was handy for official visits, but I remember many hours spent in the cellar of the Cross Keys during my initiation as a private soldier. I have never really developed the taste for beer again.

We had our lighter moments. Private Nameless loading his rifle for guard duty in the guardroom omitted to push on his safety catch and blew a hole in the tin roof. It took a lot of massaging of the ammo stock returns to cover until the next rifle range day. One of our corporals, Cpl Palmer, was reported to be leaving home several nights in uniform for extra guard duties. This ceased abruptly when he was found climbing from the bedroom window of his girlfriend when her husband returned home unexpectedly.

A sense of belonging to a large regiment was instilled by occasional battalion parades for inspection by visiting generals. During these we learned the old sweat's tricks of keeping the uniform strictly at attention and wriggling one's toes to avoid cramp. The tension was also eased by an untraceable mutter from the rear rank, 'Cor, I couldn't half strangle a Woodbine'.

Exercises became more ambitious, at first on a company scale and later at battalion strength, usually at night with most of the rank and file quite in the dark about their objectives. It was in an early night exercise that I got my only war wound. Crossing a damp ditch, I held my Lewis muzzle high to keep it out of the mud, slipped in the darkness and jabbed the back sight through my cheek into my gum. I wiped the blood off and carried on.

It was not all drill and duty. To cultivate a bit of *esprit de corps* we used to hold an annual supper and a small detachment was despatched one drill morning to a warren on the Forty Foot bank at Swineshead to collect rabbits for the supper. This necessitated the requisition of some of the rare petrol coupons allocated to B. Company. These were allocated for officer briefings and the nerve-racking officers' rounds in the middle of the night, along the riverside with masked headlamps, peering through the fog, hoping that the sentry at the next guard point would either keep his safety catch on, or finger off the trigger.

It really was a privilege having some petrol coupons because unless it was an official journey there simply was no motor travel. Towards the end of the war it was possible to relax a bit. Col. Bob Cooke fixed a battalion dance but the only way anyone could attend was to travel in an officer's car and wait five minutes at the hall while the colonel took his official muster!

There were a few serious moments. Most of our men accepted duties with a good grace, but one or two were determined not to comply. Service became compulsory and refusal was a statutory offence. A farm foreman, Freeman, was drafted to No. 4 platoon. He refused to attend, claiming his work prevented him being able to serve. His employer, D. v. Konynenburg, with a very unEnglish name, felt unable to back his excuses and Freeman was hauled before the local magistrates to 'encourage the others'.

The platoon became involved with numerous people. The local gunsmith Alf Elderkin became almost full-time armourer. Our doctor, Capt. Jim Cadas, became Company Medical Officer and turned out to be the life and soul of the company. The vicar, Mr Yeomans, served as chaplain in the RAF for the duration and his stand-in, Capt. Smith of the Church Army, kept our souls on the straight and narrow with prayers on parade when we met in the school yard behind the vicarage.

From time to time odd regular officers were drafted in to help with training, probably a R&R posting. One full colonel during the Normandy campaign was relieved of his command and posted to strengthen our sector. He felt this a disgrace, took it badly and ended it all with his revolver.

I have held back one secret about those days. Towards the middle of the war I had to organise the large platoon into two forces, one static at the bridge defence, one mobile to go to ground and harass the enemy in a roving role. Lt Marriott was in charge of the mobile unit, but I had always intended to put him in charge of the older static platoon and go off with the mobile boys myself. After all that's what command is all about.

Our valour was never tested but I like to think that in spite of being lightly armed our band of countrymen would have given a fair account of themselves.

Incidentally the spirit of the Home Guard, the patriotism, the self-sacrifice, lived on and Lt-Col Hillman White re-formed the battalion on his return from the campaigns after 1945.

Service in the Home Guard was made compulsory after 1942 for all able-bodied men not in special (reserved) occupations. Compulsion was needed to fill the gaps in the ranks as our members left to join the forces.

In the very first days of the war we saw the mass evacuation of schoolchildren and their mothers from the cities to the countryside. Trainloads of evacuees came to Lincolnshire from the East End of London. This was a tremendous social upheaval. Children and adults were taken away from their familiar surroundings and dumped straight into an unknown culture. Logistically it was a great success. Individual children or complete families were translated totally into another environment; no-one was misplaced and every one of the thousands retained their identity and their few possessions.

The logistics were splendidly organised by the civil defence authorities, ably assisted by the Women's Voluntary Service. Care was taken to keep mothers and children together as far as possible. Brothers and sisters were billeted together as much as possible and efforts were made to match the receiving hosts with the allotted evacuees. The schoolteachers were placed with the teachers they would have to work alongside. After leaving the East End in the morning whole trainloads of youngsters of all ages were placed in a fresh home before dark.

The family my mother was allocated were three young boys, the youngest under school age, from the Rackham family. It was the most she could cope with because she was already running the farmhouse, the poultry, the dairy and cooking and lodging a horseman. But it was an emergency. What blandishments had been promised to the evacuees we never found out; a holiday in the country maybe, a mixture of a Kent hopping fun time and a Southend jolly.

Anyway the reality of being dumped with total strangers who looked odd and spoke in a different kind of language must have been quite a culture shock. The reverse was even more true for the hosts. The acceptance of undisciplined rackapelts (young tearaways) whose personal habits were unusual, whose clothing was unsuitable for country living and who needed special care as they manifested signs of head lice and impetigo placed quite a strain on our quiet household.

Our boys soon adapted to the different food; clothing was found for them and they began to accept the wide open spaces, the strange men and animals and even adjusted to the privy – the earth closet down the garden path. The long walk up the lane to school quickly brought them back into touch with their fellows. One thing they could not get used to was being told what was good or bad to eat. The large Bramley apple tree in the garden bore some large green fruit which the Rackhams decided were too tempting. An hour or two later a howling stomach ache and rushes to the privy reinforced the warning about green apples.

The loneliness, the alien environment, the lack of work and loss of close family preyed on a lot of the mothers and many returned to London after a few months of rustic boredom. The children stayed longer and many left school and got jobs locally.

The prosecution of the war meant that the war effort took absolute priority. Manpower was either called up for the forces or directed into war work, coal mines, factories or food production. Locally skilled labour was diverted from farms to the sugar beet factory. Increased production was demanded from farms. Cropping instructions were issued to farmers by the county War Ags which planned the ploughing up of grassland, allocated resources – fertiliser, coal for thrashing, restricted production of bulb and flower crops. It tried to allocate timber for repairs, the few new imported ploughs and tractors and allocated labour to help harvest the crops. The surplus labour of gangs of men travelling the country seeking work soon dried up as registration and ration books drove them into factories. The local women responded nobly and helped with planting and harvesting. A Women's Land Army was created and girls from cities were fitted out with a neat and practical uniform and billeted in the villages.

We were allocated two, Kathleen and Lillian from Yorkshire, who must have found the challenge of dirty, hard, backbreaking work in all weathers a heck of a burden. They accepted it with good humour and did their best. There were quite a few humorous moments when the young women had to cope with a carthorse ten times their size. A lot of instruction was misunderstood. 'Go hoe the mangolds' could be interpreted as 'chop the mangolds up', so a lot of tuition and supervision was called for. Some of the lasses took to the life and some stayed on after the war as the wife of the farmer or farmer's son. My next-door neighbour's wife spoke with a broad Yorkshire accent when excited.

Later labour was provided by squads of prisoners of war brought out from camps. Italian POWs at one stage were allowed to billet out on farms. We had both but found that the German POW was the better worker. One in fact was so reliable and responsible at his work that when he was finally returned home, we tried to put together a gift of clothing for his family, but after six years of rationing and patching and darning, I shudder today to think of what was in that parcel.

All necessities were in short supply, timber, coal, paint, machinery and tools. Fuel was rationed. Trees became house fuel. Paraffin was allocated for tractors and petrol was rationed. About 2 gallons a week were needed for starting up the tractor and with care this could supplement the meagre car ration. When private motoring was stopped altogether even this little subterfuge came to an end. It gave us a taste of how living in the country was going to become dependent on the motor car for mobility.

Food was rationed. Almost all foods, from cheese and meat to sugar and sweets and butter. I don't recall bread or potatoes being rationed but fruit and vegetables were rationed by availability. Farmers and workers were still allowed to kill an annual pig but had to surrender their bacon coupons. Since every farm had to keep a couple of cows to supply the farm and workers with milk, these were times when the surplus milk was separated, churned and made into butter. This was a prize outside the rationing system and many short-term friends used to cycle out to the farm.

The U-boat war was sinking so much of our merchant shipping that food scarcity was a real possibility. Direct bombing on our stores and distribution networks could cut areas off at any time. It was reassuring to be told that emergency supplies were held in the district under the control of the civil authority. In our village this would be administered through the village miller and Civil Defence volunteer, Harold Garfoot.

Supplies of fresh fruit and vegetables were limited to what could be grown in this country. 'Dig for Victory' saw a spate of home gardening. Exotic fruits, oranges and bananas disappeared. Home-grown soft fruit, plums, apples and pears were in demand and acres of cabbage, carrots and onions were sent by rail to the towns. The food was plain, scarce and not particularly tempting yet everyone was quite well nourished because the act of rationing made sure that each person got his or her proper share.

Factories and metal supplies were turned over to war production. On the farms we had never had much money to purchase new machines so we had to make do with second-hand and do a lot of patching up. The blacksmith, Cyril Carter, became the key man of our machinery world – he could weld and forge broken parts. The few new and imported machines were allocated to the counties with a big area of ploughed-up grass.

I have mentioned the authority of the War Ags which operated under the Ministry of Agriculture. Another ministry which was directly involved at farm level was the

Ministry of Food. Apart from administering the rationing to every single citizen, it also controlled the purchase and supply of all foods, beef, pork, mutton, flour, sugar and fats. Appointees from the various trades graded and allocated for abattoirs all stock going through the cattle markets, and even went so far as to requisition 25 per cent of our fenland farmers' potato stocks to be stored until June to ensure supplies did not run out before the new crop was ready.

The rationing of food continued long after the war ended. In 1953 I visited the USA and was amazed to see the profusion of food, tubs of ice-cream in many flavours and T-bone steaks that hung over the sides of the platter.

Life in the village was restricted. Travel was limited. Entertainment and personal pleasures had to be subordinated to winning the war. Yet this was probably the time when everyone joined in village life and the last time when the village acted as a community. The village garden parties (for good causes like the Red Cross) were well supported. The thanksgiving service addressed by a very articulate American Army officer packed the church to the doors and made us proud to be West Pinchbeckians.

Even the government sponsored War Savings drives were a sell-out. There was nothing to spend money on – no motor cars, no house building, no foreign holidays, in fact no holidays, so towns and villages were invited to take up War Savings and buy enough War Stock to cover the cost of a tank, a destroyer or a Spitfire. The Spitfire was priced at £5,000, a bargain and we always got it.

In a way the war was kind to the village. The list of fallen was much shorter than in the First World War. My personal friends Jimmy Higham, Arnold Edinborough and Cecil Christian all returned. The village came through undamaged, just war weary. The only action within its boundaries was on a misty morning when a German aircraft, probably lost, flew alongside the River Glen towards the sea with its machine guns blazing. On another night an American plane came down in a pea field on a farm further down our lane. Once the pilot was safe, I had to muster a guard to protect it from the hares and rabbits. We were so delighted to be relieved at four in the morning by a nervous squad who had been warned we might take a potshot at them that I omitted to get them to sign for it: the only time I have had an aeroplane and I gave it away!

After the war, privation, shortages and rationing continued, but we were able to restart the Spalding Rugby Club. The playing field was behind Fulney church and is now the Coronation Channel. The headquarters for team selection, post-match baths and teas was the White Hart Hotel in the market place. The team was long on enthusiasm and not too short on skills. The leadership of George Plowman (whose forte was renderings of *Alouette, gentille Alouette*) soon welded a great team spirit and created a fluent style of play among individuals such as Jimmy Higham, Hugh King, Gordon Penrose, Doug Beba, Don Beecham, Harry Whitwell, Alex Garfoot, Don Eggleton, to name a few. This team managed a season unbeaten and took part in the absolutely shattering Notts. Sevens. Until then we thought we were fit. It was great fun and full of camaraderie.

17

Courting Days

We too were young once. We roamed the fields and hedges, the lanes and byways, explored the barns and stockyards. We knew where the birds' nests were, the dark blue misted sloes, the small hard pears. We knew which of the old inhabitants of the village could safely be taunted and which should be given a wide berth. The lad from the pub at the top of the road brought a paper packet of five Woodbines or Star to initiate us into the sinful ways of smoking and we learned that spending money only came from the sweat of the brow, from backache and sore fingers singling and weeding sugar beet for neighbours. The freedoms of the open countryside led us to new territories as we explored our friends' homes and farms. In the River Glen alongside our farm we learned to swim in spite of the cot (weeds) and mud and often had a quick dip to cool off late at night at harvest time. As very young boys we began swimming in the pools beside the river which were no more than 3 or 4 feet deep with oozy mud below. Cecil Christian got into difficulties in the weed and mud, and went under a couple of times until we managed to drag him out on to the bank, a very frightened young chap. He was more concerned that we did not inform his mother. A pity, it would have been nice to collect a life-saving medal, long before we took life-saving classes.

We developed wicked habits like stealing apples from the orchard at the end of Cooling's farm and collecting birds' eggs to blow and keep in cardboard boxes. Highly illegal today, but it did not seem to have any effect on the population of larks, hedge sparrows and yellowhammers.

Girls didn't mean much to us. We had seen them at Christmas parties, at school and at Sunday school events. They were different and they just were not interested in anything proper like football or cricket or boxing.

Bicycling up to school we went past the Monks House farm orchard where in a large straw bale shed the farm ladies were grading apples. They would often toss one over the hedge to us cheeky boys. A little further along at Monks House farmhouse, a large stone-built manor, the daughters of the house Mary and Grace Smith would be cycling to the High School. We would often chat them up or spot them as they joined 'Tiggles' Waldock along the road. Grace, the younger daughter, did not say a lot but peeped from under the broad brim of the regulation navy hat. It broke the ice and paved the way for a few visits to the cinema on Saturday nights.

The friendship developed until we were swimming in the Vernatts at Jobsons Bridge with a gang in summer and later walking through the orchard on a Sunday evening, trying to dodge her father's big car doing the rounds to plan out the next day's work.

Monks House, Spalding, c. 1930.

On my first visit for supper at Monks House in my courting days I was given a helping of a delicious cold meat pie. When it had disappeared, I was asked whether I knew what I had eaten. Everyone watched my face as I was told it was rook pie. But it was good.

In time my visits were spent half with daughter Grace and, to her chagrin, half with father Smith, who had both his boys away in the services. Bernard did not return from the Air Force; lost in a bombing raid. Father Smith needed someone to use as a talking post about his farm activities and I suppose I could offer a sympathetic ear. Later when I became officer in charge of the West Pinchbeck Home Guard platoon he found me useful because he was in charge of the Monks House platoon of the Spalding HQ company.

By the middle of 1945 the war in Europe was over and we suggested to all the parents that a wedding would be very welcome. To our surprise everything went ahead smoothly. St Bartholomew's Church at West Pinchbeck was booked, the family organisation swung into action, cakes, flowers, wedding gowns and bridesmaids' dresses were conjured up, clothing coupons were purloined for going-away outfits and family invitations were sent out. The reception was to be at Monks House in the huge kitchen. Places were limited by the size of the room and when one cancellation came in Grace and I, in the absence of her parents the hosts, offered the spare place to my Aunt Mabel but apologised that there was only room for one, no seat for her husband until someone else withdrew. What a gaffe! We never did live that social blunder down.

Charles and Ruth Smith, with their children Grace (on left), Bernard, John and Mary, c. 1936.

Brother John had not been discharged and could not get leave from the Signals Corps and brother Bernard had been posted missing, so schoolmaster, mentor and friend Arnold Bottomley stood in as best man and presented us with a heap of splendid informal photographs afterwards.

The bridesmaids looked charming: they were Grace's sister Mary, friends Rachel Turner, Ethel Ashworth and my cousin Frances Dobbs. I don't remember much about the day except the glorious summer afternoon when everyone was enjoying themselves picking ripe cherries from the tree at the back of the house.

The day ended with a third-class standing journey in the train corridor holding a first-class ticket to London, and a supper at the Strand Palace Hotel where caterpillars crawled out of the salad and we were too self-conscious to object. Honeymoon in Cornwall, cartwheeling on the sands, has left a fond feeling for the county and a secret yearning to expand our daffodil enterprise to a district where we could grow winter flowers without greenhouses.

Reginald Cecil Dobbs and Grace Smith on their wedding day, 1945.

It was now time to settle down, build a nest and raise a brood. Grace had helped on her father's farm during the war, learned the retail trade in J.T. White's fancy goods store in the Sheep Market and now helped with the office work at the Monks House farm office. Houses were in short supply but after a few months living in West Pinchbeck with my parents we were helped to get a bungalow at 139 Pennygate, which had been used by Bill and Alice Neal when Neals first got the tenancy of Monks House farm. Here we set up housekeeping and along came Richard Peter. He was born at Monks House under the strict eye of midwife Sister Julia McGuirk, who officiated for the arrival of Elizabeth and Rosemary as well.

While Richard was growing into a chubby charmer with a headful of flaxen curls we were visited by Cecil Christian, my former schoolfriend, who had spent three years as a prisoner of the Japanese after the fall of Singapore. He was still thin as a rail, never having carried much weight.

At Pennygate I was travelling to work at West Pinchbeck at first in Bernard's MG Magnette, a very classy vehicle for weekends, then when replacement parts became impossible, in a cheap Morris 8.

By 1950 my father and mother decided to move to Pode Hole, not to retire but to take a rest from the 365-day year of chores – looking after geese and chickens, milking cows night and morning, making butter every week in addition to the normal daily work of running the household and managing the farm. Father was a very strong man but suffered increasing pain from an arthritic hip which had been damaged when a horse fell on him, knocking him into a dyke. Later, in 1964, he had a hip operation in Guys Hospital. There were no ball and socket joints then; he had to have it pinned rigid, but it stopped the pain and added years to his life.

The old farmhouse was in constant need of repair. The slate roof was weathered and cracked. Bitumen sealing partly cured it but the brickwork of the walls was porous and cracked through settlement. It tended to be damp but not badly if we allowed for the lack of a damp course and the fact that there were no foundations – the walls were bedded on sand footings.

By 1956 it was obvious that extensive and expensive repairs were needed. By now the house belonged to us so we made the bold decision to knock it down and build new. We needed somewhere to live and Ted Sneath Senior kindly offered us the use of Barrowby farmhouse on the Northgate. We were used to country living but conditions were a bit primitive. The mice used to come out in the evenings and

Home Farm yard, 1937.

Home Farm, side view of the house, 1937.

The family outside the new house at Home Farm, 1966.

An aerial view of Home Farm yard, 1965.

play with Rosemary. By the end of the winter the wallpaper simply dropped off the walls and ceilings. I was ashamed to hand the house back. We could not get back to Home Farm fast enough and on 16 March 1957 moved in with no back door on and the front door unglazed, but it was great to be back.

The new house would be better and easier to run but it would still need some domestic staff. My mother had had to feed and house live-in horsemen, cope with poultry and dairy work and help out with various farm and office duties. She needed help and had a cheerful girl, Betty Watson, who was a good reliable assistant. When we moved to the old farmhouse with a young family and yard chores to do we had a live-in girl from the village, Greta, then Lillian Green, a braw lass who worked well when up but slept like the dead. Then Gwen Bright, a very thorough girl from the village shop, biked down every day. Later Mrs Hubbert, the wife of one of the farm men, came in daily and did a splendid job for years.

From then it was a steady succession of measles and chicken pox, 11+ exams, O-levels, college, school trips abroad and student exchanges until in no time at all wedding bells began to ring. Elizabeth married Bryn Chappell, the second son of county councillor Harold Chappell and Ethel of this village and settled in a new house built on their farm. Richard married Joan Cooper, daughter of Alan Cooper, a farmer from Sutton St James, and Rosemary married Steve Robinson, a lecturer from her college years at Oaklands. Now there are grandchildren and great-grandchildren.

The clock moves on.

18

Nuffield

My agricultural training was strictly practical under the instruction of Father and the methodical guidance of Grandfather. After I married, my father-in-law Charles Smith took me along to evening classes run by the then National Agricultural Advisory Service officers which gave me a grounding in theory and horticulture and sparked off an enquiring mind.

An opportunity was presented to apply for a Nuffield scholarship to travel and study overseas farming. Lord Nuffield, the car manufacturer, set up a trust which sponsored scholarships in a number of fields. The agricultural scholarships were started on a pump priming basis and are now funded by the agricultural industry and ex-scholars. The medical scholarships and research continue.

Applicants have to be between the ages of 30 and 40. At such an age they are established on a career route and they are invited to fill in an application which shows what they are doing now and asks for an outline of what subject is chosen and where they wish to pursue it.

I applied and was surprised to be successful. I believe there had so far been no scholars from this part of the country and that helped. At that time food rationing was still in force, foreign travel was forbidden by limiting the amount of available currency to £25. My chosen subject was the use of labour in arable production in America. The year was 1953 and scholars had to have some experience of farming. It was a golden opportunity, six months (travel was slower on the *Queen Mary* then) on a programme prepared by the British agricultural attaché in Washington and the US Department of Agriculture with a pocket full of dollars and a train ticket 6½ feet long.

A raw naive young villager was pitched into a new world of fresh attitudes, different economics and conditions, mingling with professors and redneck dirt farmers, researchers and settlers. I met a tremendous lot of very welcoming and helpful people, made contacts that are still ongoing today one generation further on, saw a lot, learned a little but the most valuable part of the experience was the development of myself in returning with the confidence to tackle anything within my grasp.

The journey was made possible by my father who came out of retirement to oversee the farm and by my wife who encouraged me to have a shot at it and stayed behind to look after the humdrum day-to-day business and at the same time look after three young children. Without her backing I would never have looked beyond this fen. On my return Rosemary, only two years old, didn't know me and took a while to accept me around. One look from me and her bottom lip used to curl down to her chin.

The spin-off from Nuffield can be lifelong. The contacts on the scholarship, the visits of overseas scholars to the UK carry on and meeting all these keen and forward-looking people is a mind-stimulating exercise. Annual conferences and regional seminars keep old minds in touch with new, young ideas and enthusiasms, and now every third year an international scholars' conference is held in a different host country, which is the best possible way of being educated in that country's way of life and agriculture.

19

Education in Our Industry

S hortly after returning from the States, I became involved with the National Farmers' Union – the association representative of all branches of agriculture in dealings with the government and various other authoritative bodies. At that time the Spalding district did not have a local branch but could appoint members to serve directly on the Holland County Branch executive committee. Edward Sneath Jnr was a village member of the county executive and he asked me to serve in his place. This happened at the time of the building of the new NFU offices at Camelgate, Spalding, under the new county secretary, Cliff Vivian, an ex-serving officer with the rank of major.

The Spalding area was then set up as a local branch under the chairmanship of Haydn Smith with Bertie Wray as branch secretary. I was elected vice-chairman and the branch became one of the few branches in the Holland county, joining Boston, Bourne and Wainfleet. It was one of the largest branches in the country and still is today, and has produced many of our farming leaders.

A few years' service on the county executive and I did my regulation two years in the county chair in 1980. My association with the NFU led to a few peripheral duties – a few years as a director of Agricultural Central Trading, the co-operative bulk-buying company set up by the NFU and a period of service for the Proficiency Testing organisation during its formative years. It was a controversial set-up, hated by many growers who had to pay for it, government-backed because it was a test bed for formal training in other industries. No-one in the county wanted the job and I probably did not help my public career by trying to get a sensible training scheme off the ground in the face of opposition.

Fifty years ago a young man willing to learn farming could become a 'farm pupil', which sounded better than 'apprentice'. His father would select a tutor farmer, pay an annual premium of £100 and the lad would join the staff to see all the operations and learn at the foot of the master. He was unpaid, a supernumerary, did not have to take his turn at every job rough or smooth, and such pupils as I met depended very much on the calibre of their host farmer.

The workers were trained by the senior men – the head horseman, head tractor driver, head cowman or farm foreman – and as a matter of personal pride and status they made a good job of hammering craft skills into their charges. Alongside this system of learning the hard way there existed a formal system of apprenticeship where certain country crafts, notably shepherding, gamekeeping and so on, were taught by the craftsman for three years to an apprentice on a low wage who then should be able to go out and secure a better-paid position.

After the war ended in 1945 it became apparent that new skills were needed in farming. Workers needed to be knowledgeable with animals, able to operate new machines and understand new fertilisers and chemicals. It was not going to be good enough to be just strong in the arm and weak in the head. A widespread apprenticeship scheme was brought in for agriculture with lower wages during training, rewarded by a premium on passing out after three years.

Very soon a formal Agricultural Training Board was set up – a test bed for training boards for other industries. I got involved with the ATB at its inception. As a member of the Holland County NFU executive I was pushed into chairing the county ATB committee by Harry Caudwell, chairman of the county NFU and Cliff Vivian, secretary, who could probably see a rough ride ahead and needed a fall guy. Anyway after a fitful start training became accepted as a necessary evil and my involvement included proficiency testing, taking examinations and writing new tests.

The ATB was financed by contributions from farmers and in the formative years by government grant to cover office costs. It provided training in two ways. It continued a formal three-year apprenticeship on farms and involved the farm colleges in providing short courses. In order to assess the progress of students and apprentices, the proficiency testing scheme set up by the Young Farmers' movement was used and eventually taken over. The proficiency testing service was kept independent and on a very practical level. A weakness was that it could be tailored to a specialist employer's particular crop and needs, though it was still a certificate of practical ability.

Apprenticeship was now in the realm of the experts and like all good educationalists, the experts soon began to alter and improve. They introduced a New Entrants Scheme, then a Youth Training Scheme. Quite where they have got to today no-one knows but the time is ripe to reintroduce an apprenticeship scheme which everyone understands.

Not all workers like the idea of proficiency testing but since the Agricultural Wages Board recognises the tests and sets a higher wage for craftsmen it is worth making the effort. There is now a wage structure for agriculture and all trainees receive the normal wage during training and are paid to go on courses.

This led to an interest in the teaching of farm skills and agricultural theory at our county colleges of further education. Holland County Council was late in setting up its Boston College of Further Education and when it decided to widen the college with a unit at Holbeach for agriculture I got roped in. The chairman of the county council, Harold Chappell, was a very wily operator. His chief critic over the cost of the college, Councillor Case, was appointed chairman of governors and became its greatest proponent. Hearing of the Holbeach centre proposal, I chatted to Harold (my daughter's father-in-law) with a few ideas about what was needed. Before I could turn round I found myself a governor of the college with special responsibilities for the Holbeach centre.

This interest has lasted forty years and has carried on to see the Holbeach centre amalgamated into the new Lincolnshire agricultural college alongside Caythorpe and

Riseholme Colleges in 1974. It has seen the colleges provide part-time and full-time courses, seen the widening of the scope of courses to include equestrian, small animal, gamekeeping and countryside courses. The number of students has increased from a mere two or three hundred to over a thousand and good residential accommodation is now provided. During my last year as a governor the Lincolnshire college of agriculture became the School of Agriculture of De Montfort University, Leicester, and students can enrol to take a series of courses which lead to a degree or HND qualification.

The governors agonised long and hard over joining in with De Montfort, but a decision was needed, the other participating universities offered nothing for our agricultural students and the Lincoln campus was still a dream for the future with a shortfall of £30m in funding. The principal introduced a degree course in golf and I thought it time to leave.

20

Farm Expansion

The war years saw all spare pasture ploughed for cropping. Potato growing was made compulsory by the War Ag. and labour shortages were met by recruiting Land Army girls and later prisoners of war. For the first time in our lives the crops produced earned money which was hard to spend because there were no goods or equipment to be purchased. The habit of careful husbandry saw Father able to buy his farm before he died at the huge price of £100 per acre in 1950.

At the end of the war farmers had to keep books of account and have stocktakings and audits in place of the old Schedule B system under which they paid income tax according to the rateable value of their land. This new double-entry book-keeping was pushed my way, though the filing system remained the equivalent of a pile of receipted bills impaled on a length of bent wire for years to come.

Richard, the third generation, now has computerised field records and accounts which can give him a trial balance at the press of a button. People laugh at my calculations on the back of an envelope but I still swear by it for farming. If you haven't got a figure at the back of your head for the value of your cash balance and unsold stocks that is within 10 or 15 per cent of what you actually achieve you can't begin to cost out the next project or land purchase. If the proposal does not give you a potential profit margin of at least 25 per cent it is not worth the risk of facing the dangers of pests, diseases or falling market prices.

The Nuffield scholarship saw me come home full of ideas. By now we were living in the farmhouse; parents had moved to Pode Hole. Neighbour Harold Smith was giving up Rectory Farm at Guthram, 80 acres of hungry silt full of eelworm and twitch but it had potential. The feoffees of Spalding Church, swayed by my keenness no doubt, rented it to me for 30s an acre. R.T. Proctor, an esteemed feoffee, riled me on his second visit by saying, 'Well, it looks as if we shall get the rent this year.' But of course it was a farmer's compliment.

Monks House farm came vacant in 1960 and was offered to me. This gave us 150 more acres to deal with of which 40 were in fruit orchards. Here we met a whole raft of new people. Harry Green the steam cultivator driver, Charlie Woods the horseman of the old school, Charlie Taylor, Bill Pearson, always wrapped in a woollen scarf winter and summer and the best of the lot, Father Box. He was a quiet capable artisan, who cared for a crippled wife without complaining, and repaired and fixed everything on the farm to do with horses, carpentry and forge.

In trying to restore the orchards to productivity I enlisted the help of Mr Flack of

Cropping outdoor daffodils on Guthram farm, 1994.

Cropping indoor daffodils in the mobile glasshouse at Monks House farm, 1965.

Lifting daffodils, Mill Green, 1993.

Whaplode, a retired fruit foreman. At the age of 70 he was a fruit craftsman supreme, as enthusiastic as a 20-year-old, and he shamed me with his agility. In spite of his inspiration, care and tuition at the end of the day we had to admit that economics, climate, tree layout and structure were just totally unsuitable in a modern (1965) age and we had to grub the orchard and turn it to arable. However, the greenhouses started us expanding our flower bulb section. The occupation of the greenhouses increased our need for bulbs and we added daffodils to the cropping, especially for forcing. This eventually built up to 15 acres of tulips and 20 of daffodils at that time.

In about 1970 margins in farming were getting tight. Brother-in-law John Smith was tenant of Drainage Farm, some 240 acres at Bourne Fen. The Black Sluice Internal Drainage Board wanted to sell it and offered it to John as tenant. John could not find the £42,000 needed and asked if I was interested. After a lot of discussion we used our savings to raise a bank loan to purchase it.

Our venture into the drummy, black and gravelly soils of Bourne Fen brought us into contact with Charlie Ashby, farm foreman. Charlie had been trained by Ben Smith, John's uncle, and knew more about farming the fen than John and me put together. He kept his counsel but must have been amused at some of our antics. There were short acquaintances with Dick Andrew, ram-headed when we needed a bit of push, Albert and Geordie Kilbon, unfailing optimists, Norman Seymour, left too long undisciplined, and a very pleasant engagement with Tom Goode, a braw strong machine operator who could divine our farm policy and needs, with merely a few words of suggestion, not instruction.

A year or two later the Dearnley boys at Mill Green decided to sell up and put Obvallaris Farm on the market. It failed to reach reserve price and was withdrawn. I heard about it and knew a lot of it was best quality silt. I briefed our solicitors, Maples, to put in an offer and after a bit of 'secret' negotiation when the auctioneers had no idea of the identity of the client, I managed to buy it for £500 an acre. A ridiculous price on the day but cheap two years later.

A few fields were added within our effective operating area of 6 miles until Edward Sneath wanted to build a retirement bungalow on one of our fields at Tydd Road. By exchanging fields with a cash adjustment we then took over Leaveslake Farm.

Changes have taken place. The major change is in the number of workers. Five full-time workers now look after every operation – the number that it would have needed to service any one of the farms absorbed. The cropping also has been simplified. We have concentrated on producing arable crops, daffodil bulbs and flowers. Land is hired out for vegetable growing and we have tried to avoid dependency on 'easy' combinable crops. Long term we have bet on crops which are not easy to grow – perhaps we shall be proved right!

During all these years that I have been trying to create a better farm business Grace did a fantastic job of bringing up and training our family by example. Life has not always been easy. Our first kitchen cupboards were made from orange boxes and money for home or family had to be wrung from a demanding farm budget. The army training manual said 'Make do and mend' and for the early years we had to do just that. She managed the household; she kept our feet on the ground. Richard won a place at the Grammar School; I thought it would be great if he could go to Oundle to start the education I had missed. He flunked (maybe deliberately?) the entrance exam but mother saw that the upbringing was right. At Caythorpe Agricultural College doing what he wanted he passed out with a good diploma and in some way has since developed characteristics of judgement, leadership, tact and compassion that were never in his paternal genes.

The same careful nurturing has come through in Elizabeth and Rosemary. Both decided the type of practical college courses they wanted at Aylesbury and Oaklands and have devoted their lives to bringing up their families exactly as their mother did and to helping their husbands develop their careers and businesses. They all live within a few miles and if I can say it without tempting fate they all work together as a family. Each one respects the qualities of the others.

Life Off-farm

I served on the South Holland Horticultural Association which represented the growers of tulips and daffodils and the local glasshouse industry. In those days the SHHA was a vibrant enterprising group which was accepted in London and the Ministry of Agriculture as representative of the bulb industry – and in those days tulips and daffodils were a very large part of the national flower trade from December until mid-May. The SHHA had ideas and did things. It was blessed with a very forward-looking steersman in Cliff Vivian, its secretary, and organised first the Spalding Flower Parade and later the Springfields show gardens in 1966. Cliff Vivian was also involved in organising the planning and promotion of a very large co-operative marketing proposal which would handle all the horticultural output from South Lincolnshire. After months of discussion (South Lincs. held more merchants for produce to the square mile than any other district) the drop-outs left two groups, about twenty brassica growers who set up ELGRO at Kirton for vegetables and twenty-odd growers who started Selected Growers Ltd to market flower bulbs and tomatoes in 1966. This last was a co-operative begun with government encouragement and a grant. The office was in the NFU building, the manager engaged was a Dutchman Kees Bot and the warehouse was hired from a potato merchant in his off-season. Trading was with the firms and customers passed on by the members.

Before long land was acquired at Weston from Jim Tatchell, a director; a warehouse was built for packing and shipment and a wooden office erected. The grants began to run out after a couple of years; the charges levied barely covered expenses and some drastic measures were needed. I had been asked to serve on the board and after a stormy meeting or two, I, as vice-chairman to Francis Hanson, was asked to take charge. This was one of the turning points in our family life. I judged that this task would take a lot of my time and at a family board meeting son Richard, at the early age of 23, agreed to start taking over certain management duties on the farm. This freed me to take an almost daily interest in the business at Weston. We now had a new manager, Bob Out, also a Dutchman, who got to grips with finding new customers, setting up pre-packing lines and running the business. Where I felt he needed help was in restoring the confidence of members, which was at a low ebb. I had to renegotiate the marketing agreements to create some financial stability and get members' acceptance of the new rules. This meant a fair bit of legwork and more diplomacy than I had in me, but we got approval. In order to justify the good faith of members' support, I spent a lot of time at Weston, not interfering with management, rather protecting the management from interference from directors and members who all had different and better ideas of how the business should be run. I tried to be a support to the management and to demonstrate to growers that someone cared about this section of their business: a sort of public relations job.

The business progressed; trade built up in pre-packing for the expanding super-markets. Bob Out's quiet ability developed the export market and the company name was changed to Lingarden, a much more meaningful title in any language. The trading was broadened to include bulb machinery, vegetables and particularly onions, and after a few abortive starts flower marketing has been developed to export cut daffodils as well as bulbs all over Europe and North America. Membership now extends down to Kent and Cornwall and even into Eire. I joined Lingarden in 1966 and after serving on the board for twenty-five years retired in 1992. I served as chairman of the board until 1975 and rather unkindly remained on the board for over a decade. This connection with Lingarden led to other jobs. During this time I served on the executive of the South Holland Horticultural Association to make sure that Lingarden's interests were catered for but was never invited to take office. By the time I retired in 1993 the committee seemed to be run from a distant office, and to take less interest in the local industry. At times in my last years I even had to ask for bulb matters to be included on the agenda!

My involvement with Lingarden led to membership of the Springfields Council. This had been set up by the NFU to promote the British bulb industry and some local big guns had been involved – Len van Geest, Willis White, Dick Heath, Francis Hanson, Percy Taylor, Ted Grant and of course the ubiquitous Cliff Vivian as the expeditor. The show gardens were laid down in 1966 and provided an attraction for the thousands of visitors at tulip time. The tulip fields were often headed by the time of the flower parade and for reasons of rotation the fields were often far from the roads of the tulip route. The gardens provided named plantings of flower bulbs for visitors to stroll round and admire at their leisure. The administration of the flower parade had been carried on voluntarily by NFU staff; now that a show garden had been added the administration was handed over to a council of appointed bulb growers with a separate office and staff. My involvement with Lingarden led to an invitation to join the Springfields council, and during a reshuffle I was appointed deputy to Len van Geest, the original chairman. On Len's death I became chairman responsible for the show gardens, the flower shows, related events and for the general promotion and publicity for the bulb industry. This included the flower parade with which I had been connected from the first, through the YFC and later the West Pinchbeck village float.

If I had to choose a failure in my life work, it would have to be my efforts for the bulb industry. For the last thirty years irreversible changes have taken place. The spring festival and parade has to face up to competition from many other new attractions. For financial success the parade needs a closed circuit with entry by ticket. No circuit is available in Spalding. The support, both material and financial, for the gardens and the parade comes from growers as well as commercial firms.

Queen Elizabeth the Queen Mother opening Springfields Gardens, 17 April 1986.

During this time the acreage of tulips has dwindled from 1,500 to less than 50 (no longer recorded as a separate crop by MAFF) and the acreage of daffodils has increased to over 12,000. Clearly there is a need to promote the industry as it exists today to gain the support and involvement of hundreds of growers. My efforts to change the thrust of policy over to daffodils fell on deaf ears – unfortunately I lost my majority and resigned.

My close involvement with Lingarden also led to an invitation to join the advisory committee at the Horticultural Research Station at Kirton. This station was in those days run by the Ministry of Agriculture which had taken it over from the Holland County Council. Its remit was to conduct research of a practical nature on the bulb and vegetable crops grown in the area. This was an absorbing appointment, bringing contact with both practical horticultural officers and long-haired scientists on basic research, as well as civil service types from the ministry. I must have outstayed my welcome at Kirton because after serving my three terms or more as a committee member under Ted Grant, I was asked to follow him into the chair for over the three terms again up to the incorporation in HRI (Horticultural Research Institute – later HR International).

This led to a splendid education in the workings of government departments, policy makers and civil servants, to contacts in business and research all over the country because chairmen were invited to meet permanent secretaries and even ministers, to meet the other chairmen of research units and inspect the network of research units from Yorkshire down to Cornwall and the Isles of Scilly. It was a tremendous opportunity to get to know a vast team of dedicated experts in both the research and commercial fields and make friendships which are alive to this day.

Kirton led to an opportunity to sit as a bulb grower member on the board of the Glasshouse Crops Research Institute. In those days GCRI in Sussex had the task of providing basic research for bulbs as well and had close contact with Kirton. Apart from the boffins on the staff, the board itself was a pretty eclectic lot, university professors of abstruse disciplines, leaders of the tomato, mushroom and chrysanthemum business, a high-powered bunch but thankfully with enough charm and smalltalk to make even a fen man feel welcome.

At that time the Agricultural Research Council controlled and funded our research. It kept in touch with progress and the industry's needs by appointing JCOs – Joint Consultative Organisations, which sat every four years. I sat on one for ornamentals under Martin Slocock and when the next one came due I had to chair it. How wonderful to be given the whole cornucopia of research to dip into for your industry but how difficult to select what is really vital and affordable (and how interesting to have to chop down the mischievous committee member to size).

The JCO brought contacts with senior undersecretaries in the ministry, visits to Kew and its genetic bank, Brogdale, for tissue culture and so on and eventually out of the blue a letter from 10 Downing Street stating archaically that 'Her Majesty has it in mind to make you an officer of the Order of the British Empire'. The letter arrived in a pile of farm mail and Richard opened it and just managed to keep it under his hat. Eventually the day of glory arrived and Grace and daughters Elizabeth and Rosemary took the train with me in all our finery to Buckingham Palace. Many memories fade, but still strong are the sight of the guards, swords drawn, rigid at the salute, the smooth meticulous organisation, the patient personal attention of the Queen to recipients and, a light touch, the background music coming from the rear of the hall proved on closer examination to be provided by a guards' band in the gallery.

Another job which came through the NFU connection was with Lingrain, a co-operative marketing group for grain. Haydn Smith, I and about a dozen farmers in South Lincs. held discussions, exploratory talks and feasibility studies and eventually set up the company. After a tentative start, a good track record was set up and many fence-sitters began to join. Offices were set up in 1979 in the NFU building at Spalding, expanded to fill a couple of rooms at Lingarden and eventually moved to a purpose-built office and boardroom at the silos on Boston Docks. The silos and export facility followed a short-lived export warehouse at the Sutton Bridge Dock where the owner wanted total control after we had given his venture some credibility. The Boston silos expanded to fill the site and a further export facility was built at Immingham to give access to 10,000-ton vessels. A few ventures into shipping, malt trading and importing were tried. Now the original company has amalgamated with Wold grain and has over 118 farmer members and a total throughput of more than 300,000 tons. I served as vice-chairman to Haydn Smith from 1979 to 1988. Since I was a year older than the chairman it seemed wise to nurse a younger board member along in readiness.

The decade 1980–90 brought another interest. The Holland Lincs. NFU had always presented two district members for the Potato Marketing Board. John Carter died in office and as potatoes had always been a serious part of our business, I was nominated as replacement. I had been about a bit but the first meeting I had to attend was at Hans Crescent in London, the next was in Edinburgh. The next ten years were spent all over the country one or two days a week. I had never taken expenses for my NFU or research duties but I quickly had to be pragmatic and cover the huge cost of travel by claiming the standard expenses. This was a whole different crowd of people: 90 per cent of them enthusiastic, friendly and knowledgeable. It was possible to pick out an interesting mix of place sitters, semi-politicos playing the game for re-election and partisans who were taking the narrow view of fighting for their particular sector to the exclusion of all else.

The duties were onerous, the demands of local potato growers insatiable but it was a stimulating time in the company of keen minds and tough businessmen. I particularly enjoyed serving on the research committee which provided contact with a whole new battalion of researchers from Cambridge, Sutton Bridge, Long Ashton and Scotland. What was an especial privilege was meeting all the young postgraduate researchers that the PMB was able to sponsor on their first PhD project.

The government determined in its wisdom that freedom of trade was the new policy, managed markets were out of order and the PMB would have to undergo a radical change. Coming off the PMB, where commitment to duties was regular and demanding, left a gap in my life with no immediate duty in view.

I was able to help out more in the day-to-day routine of the farm and the businesses of my sons-in-law, and after chasing all over England and Scotland for research and PMB and developing a taste for overseas travel – Holland with Lingarden, the continent and Canada with the PMB – I began to look to explore the antiquities which I had last studied at school. In the company of son-in-law Steve, daughter Rosemary or one or two of the grandchildren, I have been able to visit Rome, Pompeii, Athens, Crete, Rhodes, Cyprus, Egypt and Turkey. Hopefully this broadened their view of the world as well as mine. With the pressure of business off it has been possible to join the Nuffield Scholars' three-yearly international conference in Australia and Canada – wonderful farm technology, dynamic farmers, amazing scenery and great people both in the country visited and within the party.

The last body with which I served was the local drainage board – the Welland & Deepings Internal Drainage Board. This board manages the drainage of our whole district except the actual rivers. Our daily life and business in the fens is totally dependent on good drainage and I firmly believe that with local knowledge and good engineers the drainage here is effected as cheaply and efficiently as possible. The only caveat is that river maintenance and coastal flood protection is the responsibility of persons and bodies far distant and not personally at risk.

I do have a personal hobby, and that is scribbling – not a lot and not very well but it oozes out like sap from a wound in a tree. It started in the dim and distant past when a school friend, Peter Tombleson, came back from National Service in Palestine with the Parachute Regiment. He had to find a niche in civilian life and became the editor of the local newspaper, the *Spalding Guardian*. He had a countryside circulation and asked me to do a farming column. This I did for many years anonymously under the title of 'Fenland Farming Notes', in which I recounted the tribulations and triumphs of growing potatoes, wheat and mangolds in those times. Peter moved elsewhere in the newspaper group and somehow I got taken over by David Young, the editor of the *Spalding Free Press*, for whom I contributed a weekly piece under the byline of Harvester. This was a labour of love, part-technical with all the latest wheezes and varieties, part-political (blame the government) and part-old country philosophy. A labour of love because after working all day I would sit down at 10 p.m. to bash out next week's column before the deadline. David must have liked it; he got a cartoonist to liven up the subheadings, advertised it as a special feature and even paid me £1.50 a week. When the rate went up to £3 and I got a heap of offcuts for copy paper I thought this is the life of Riley. I remember when I declared this wonderful income to the Inland Revenue I tried to claim expenses because I subscribed to a few specialist journals to keep one step behind progress, if not up with it. The claim was disallowed and I have never thought much of the fair judgement of our tax collectors since.

22

Spalding Tulip Parade

One winter's night a group of village growers had a visit from Adrianus van Driel, the parade designer, who mesmerised us in our kitchen to convince us that we should enter a village flower float the coming year. After a couple of sceptical meetings van Driel's enthusiasm fired us to have a go. We were worried about the cost but after I put up an underwriting of £175 if needed we set out to raise the funding through whist drives and raffles. For many years the West Pinchbeck tulip float was built in one of our sheds by welder Noel Bellamy, assisted by Roland Alexander, Maurice Chappell, Hardy Rigby, Hugh Gotobed and others. The framework was built during dark winter evenings; the cladding of rye straw mats

Heading tulips for parade floats, 1996.

Edward Sneath driving Percherons for West Pinchbeck village float in the Spalding Tulip Parade, 1966.

was stitched into place by our volunteers. Two days before the parade day in early May our float was towed to Stan Tipler's sheds in Northgate, a more central point. There the float committee men, their wives and children and helpers pinned on the tulip heads, stitched the muslin and taffeta flags and wings and consumed fish and chip suppers until the job was finished late on Friday night.

Early on the Saturday morning a tractor pulled the float to the Fisherman's Arms at Pode Hole, horse-shafts were put on the front and Edward Sneath in garish costume drove with a spruce beribboned team of Percherons up to the parade. This continued for many years. It was a village effort. Many of the helpers had no connection with the bulb industry. Ours was the only village to have a regular entry and we could look with disdainful pride at other villages which could only manage an entry for one year. After about fifteen years, Maurice Chappell and I collected a list of other duties so that our physical contribution was curtailed and eventually this village project was dropped.

When the village started entering a float in the Spalding Tulip Parade it seemed a brilliant idea to get Ed Sneath's horses to pull it round the parade route – almost the only ones in the parade. Ed was as enthusiastic as we were and readily agreed to don whatever costume was appropriate, be it Turkish pantaloons and fez or coachman's

Village float in Spalding Tulip Parade.

livery and tricorne. He was always accompanied by Perce Darley, his groom, smartly got up in brown leggings and brown bowler hat. Much elbow-grease was expended on shining the harness brasses before the parade and an early morning start saw the tails and manes properly plaited and tied with red and yellow ribbon. It was a great sight for the thousands of visitors to Spalding.

Sadly Edward passed to the great stable in the sky in 1995. He would have been delighted that his coffin was drawn to the church by a team from old rival Michael Hemfrey, and honoured that the team was Percherons.

There are no horses on the Money Bridge farm today. But I always look across the fields as I go past, seeking the reassurance of those great, majestic creatures.

23

Young Farmers

An activity which began soon after the end of the war was Young Farmers' Clubs. There were none in the county at the time but we had heard of them flourishing in Devon and the south-west. Around our farm kitchen table (the farmhouse kitchen is the powerhouse, boardroom and executive office for progress), Peter Scarr, Alex Garfoot and I talked it over and decided that there was a need for one. We were all over the stipulated age limits (12 to 25) but what did that matter?

We founded the Spalding & District YFC, recruited the Tidswell youngsters from Surfleet, the Fletcher boys, Margaret Culpin, Maxine Holmes, Ina Rowell, John and Mildred Richardson and the Seymour girls from Moulton and the club was away. We set up a programme of talks by specialists, visits to leading farms and nearby factories. After a short time we became more ambitious. We (I was the secretary) organised a rally at the West Pinchbeck school and playing field when other clubs were formed in the county. We organised public meetings alongside ministry advisers and invited speakers with a national reputation to address us and farmers generally on current topics.

The district was inundated with visitors for three weekends at tulip time and there was nothing organised for them. The Young Farmers with the brashness of youth 'borrowed' the large Auction Hall in Spalding, asked for bulb equipment from suppliers and growers and laid on an exhibition on tulip growing which showed the botany, husbandry and machinery involved in growing bulbs and forcing winter flowers. All this was displayed around a colourful centrepiece mosaic of tulip heads. The admission charge and the descriptive programme cost the princely sum of threepence.

The club progressed to take part with a float in the Spalding Flower Parade when it started and was granted the right to sell teas at the display on the Halley Stewart field. Some nearby clubs have faded but Spalding YFC still enters its own home-made float in the parade and still lays on teas and refreshments for visitors. It is one of the richest clubs in the UK because of its hard work on those teas. The club now raises funds for charities, especially with its big firework and bonfire display at Guy Fawkes time.

There is a clear contrast between the young people who simply ask for entertainment and amusement to be provided for them and the Young Farmers' movement which organises its own activities. They have a lot of fun and dances as well but have always carried on a programme of learning. The early days were very

Reg, the Young Farmer, 1943.

Young Farmers' Club Agricultural Display Float, c. 1951.

much taken up with proficiency testing and farm skills such as sugar beet gapping and singling or dressing poultry for the table. A lot of that has disappeared but the clubs provide a good training for life. A lot of the members pair off in marriage (it's called a marriage bureau) and many ex-members use the experience of running a club, holding office and organising, to move to responsible positions in society later.

I have a very soft spot for the enthusiasms of the YFCs. So I should have, as I am also a member. I was granted life membership of the Spalding YFC after many years on its Advisory Committee. Not bad being a young farmer at the age of eighty-six!

*Young Farmers'
Club Agricultural
Display Float,
c. 1951.*

Afterword

Today, I look back over the most astounding changes in the countryside, from horses reigning supreme with the whole culture based on the care and use of these noble creatures to the mechanical systems of present times when farming is not an art and skill but a blend of applied science, chemistry, sophisticated genetics, still needing a special kind of human input however.

Some things never change, the interference of political decisions, but the weather still dominates our daily life and our results. Our government can now control every field and hedgerow, dictate how much land we can sow, and has drawn up a new map of the whole country in far greater detail than the Domesday Book. We have been nationalised.

I have tried to play a part in improving the marketing, the scientific developments and the training of young people with limited success. But I still enjoy seeing the enthusiasm of Young Farmers and the new generations of Nuffield scholars.

I have proudly seen Father's smallholding of 30 acres grow to 1,400 acres of farmed land and can still enjoy helping to keep the farm going by doing odd jobs such as pulling (not sowing!) wild oats and tidying up the beet rows and potato row ends.

But best of all, son Richard carries on and does a better job of farming than I ever could.

Reg and son Richard, 2006.